CW00403200

INSIDE

INSIDE

Jane Kelly

THE
SOCIAL
AFFAIRS
UNIT

© The Social Affairs Unit 2009
All rights reserved

British Library Cataloguing in Publication Data
A catalogue record of this book is available from the British Library

All views expressed in this publication are those of the author, not
those of the Social Affairs Unit, its Trustees, Advisers or Director

Printed and bound in the United Kingdom

ISBN-13: 978-1-904863-40-3

Social Affairs Unit
314–322 Regent Street
London W1B 5SA
www.socialaffairsunit.org.uk

The Social Affairs Unit has no responsibility for the persistence or
accuracy of URLs for websites referred to in this publication, and does
not guarantee that any content on such websites is, or will remain,
accurate or appropriate.

*For Londoners, inside and out.
All names have been changed to
protect the guilty.*

ABOUT THE AUTHOR

Jane Kelly was born in Charlton, south-east London in 1956, adopted and taken to live in Staffordshire. She took a degree in History at Stirling University and taught English for a year at the University of Sosnowiec in southern Poland. In 1980, she won the Cosmopolitan Magazine Young Journalist competition and returned to London as a freelance.

She was on the dole for three years and did a variety of jobs including auxiliary nursing. In 1983, she was runner-up in the Catherine Pakenham Award for women journalists. She then found work on *The Telegraph*, *The Times*, and the *London Evening Standard*, and then joined the staff of *The Mail on Sunday*. She left there two years later to work on the *Today* newspaper, then freelanced before she became a staff feature writer on *The Daily Mail*, where she remained for fifteen years. She has also written for *The Spectator*.

Since leaving the *Mail* in 2004, she has freelanced for many papers, gained half a teaching qualification and has written a biography of the actor Colin Farrell. *Inside* is her second published book.

Jane is a member of the Stuckist painters, who favour using paper, paint and canvas rather than sump oil and cows in formaldehyde. Jane lives in West London with her cat Brenda, several rats in the shed and some visiting slugs in the hall.

1

At 8.45 a.m. a prison officer appeared and shouted: 'Get ready peeps – they're 'ere!' There was a noise like a football crowd or an excited mob rushing towards us, and the brightly lit, green-painted corridor was suddenly packed with men from all over the planet jostling, shouting and laughing. The officer's cry launched 'free flow', when prisoners flow – or rather surge – up from the wings into the Education Department and the teaching day starts.

Prisons vary across London; there are more Afro-Caribbeans in HMP (Her Majesty's Prison) Brixton, more Asians in Pentonville. Wormwood Scrubs sits within the Heathrow catchment area so it holds between eighty and 112 nationalities at any time. In order of numbers: Nigeria, Jamaica and Somalia, with Ireland and Poland following.

Of all foreign-national prisoners, 13 per cent of all UK convicts, 45 per cent are concentrated in London, or 'Lagtown' as it might now be called. One in five she-lags up in HMP Holloway are also foreign nationals.

Clutching photocopied pages of poetry, feeling laughably tiny, I stood in this mêlée, squeezed between Nigerians on remand, still able to wear flowing traditional dress, looking like delegates to the UN, clusters of old Muslims with long beards and tiny Astrakhan hats, young jihadists, in robes and sandals. There were smiling Vietnamese, with pudding-basin haircuts and shirts with little stand-up collars and buttons down the side, and gloomy Estonians, Russians and Poles.

In the suffocating dust and heat of the corridor, men chattered and shouted in Yoruba, Ibo and Polish with a constant undertone of Caribbean patois. While nearly half the prisoners were foreign, the rest were mainly black Brits, pouring into prison through the cracks in our broken society.

I watched Rasta men strolling the corridor in big groups, sporting elaborate hairstyles with intricate patterns of shaving, knotting and combing. In prison, hairdressing is one alternative to playing with Game Boys and watching reality TV. Some of the dreadlocks were so old they were rotting and gave off a strange musty odour.

Many of the black boys who'd been sentenced wore grey tracksuit bottoms pulled down under their sharply defined buttocks, a bizarre style which apparently began in US gaols to indicate that an inmate was available for sex. It is unlikely that they knew this, as these black prisoners were notoriously homophobic.

At the distant end of the corridor, I caught the very rare sight of a white man in prison. Not just white-skinned but at least seventy years old, sitting on a low stool painting Islamic-looking murals in a sickly pink on the wall outside the art room. He stood up and greeted me warmly.

'Old Frank', a pensioner originally from Barnsley in Yorkshire, had been working on these walls for a year. He hadn't been provided with any varnish, so the ones he finished had to be covered with sheets of brown paper to protect them from cigarette burns and graffiti.

The art room where I was to spend my time was large with dingy unpainted walls. Most art rooms look rough, but there was something particularly desolate about this one, and I was going to be in it for over two and a half hours, morning and afternoon, trying to inspire people.

'As it's your first day, they will play you up,' said Mr Barno Nusrat cheerfully. Of mixed Caribbean and Chinese origin, a regular prison officer in the Education Department, he looked kind, but I was quickly warned that he reported teachers for even small infractions of the rules. He would also bribe men, befriend them, turning on an act of being a fellow Caribbean, but then incite them, turn on them angrily and haul them back to the cells if he was in that kind of mood.

'Whatever happens I will back you up. If you want me to get rid of anyone, just say the word,' he said, stretching his mouth into a very long smile which seemed almost flirtatious, as ten black Brits and a pair of scrawny white twins slouched in scowling at me.

It was my first day in HMP Wormwood Scrubs as a teacher, but the night before I had been at the Scream Gallery, owned by Rolling Stones guitarist and painter Ronnie Wood, acting out the remains of my career as a journalist.

I'd been to the opening of an exhibition by a young English gent (Harrow, Harvard, Heatherley's, the expensive private art school in Chelsea), who painted glamorised versions of famous artists' studios, from Picasso's in Paris to Gauguin's in Tahiti. More significantly, he sold these brightly coloured works to A-list Hollywood stars.

No one was there to look at his paintings. Guests mostly milled about in the centre of the room, backs firmly to the walls, before spilling out onto the pavement, facing one way and squinting their eyes in the fading light, past the roofs of parked cars, searching up the street for just one faint glimpse of Kate Moss.

Rumour said she might turn up, but her wraith-like form did not manifest. Back inside I was squashed between the artist's shipping-heiress mother and Pierce Brosnan, the former James Bond. He told me he was filming a musical with Meryl Streep at Pinewood. 'I've still got it you know,' he said as if there was some doubt. 'I can still dance.'

Breaking out of that conclave, I came face to face with one of Ron Wood's charming children. He began spilling out details of recent family holidays with the Jaggers and cosy, communal drug-taking among the elite rock families. This was a dream situation for any journalist: to be nose to wounded nose with a naive child who knows too much and can't shut up.

There is something about me that encourages people to talk, and I once played with the idea that being a journalist was similar to being a therapist, until I went to a therapist and realised that therapy is about trust whilst journalism is all about betrayal.

Over the years, I had become squeamish about what I was doing, but I wrote down everything the boy said anyway. It was worth £80 in a tabloid diary, and another paper might pick it up. There was always the buzz of that possibility – even though I knew I was no longer a journalist, I was changing my career, becoming a teacher, a worthy member of society with a respectable moderate income. But a journalist is like a serial killer: it's just something in you, and every now and then you just have to do another, you need the excitement of your crimes, even though they may be committed years apart.

When I was twenty-five, twenty-five years ago, I came to London to be a journalist. I didn't know anyone or have anywhere to live, but in my red-striped babygro and Kickers I walked into rumbling, crumbling offices on Fleet Street, with their nicotine-stained walls and criminaloid editors, and I quickly found people willing to give me work.

A surprising number of those editors were other go-getting, ruthless young women from the provinces in expensive asymmetrical haircuts and Lycra skirts, often worn with no knickers underneath. We were all eager for risk, and Mrs Thatcher, for all her later megalomania, had opened a window of opportunity – or at least had bent back the bars to let some of us scramble through. I was still a clodhopper from the provinces, and people let me know it, but I didn't care because my money was as good as theirs and my talent was as good or better.

For the next quarter of a century I was out to lunch. We'd go out as an office, or at least as a department, to the Savoy River Room. The Editor took favoured employees and putative mistresses to the Grill. We'd wave across at Cecil Parkinson or Princess Margaret. I'd spend my evenings and sometimes whole nights in Soho.

But over that time our great profession changed; the NUJ and the once-powerful SOGAT, with its retinue of powerfully coiffed secretaries, vanished. They somehow weakened and melded; pretty vacuous secretaries became writers on low pay. Freelance writers were put on reduced pay or not used at all. Papers were coming out with less and less real writing. We were into the age of 'churnalism'.

Our office, once a friendly, untidy place with desks piled up like Mexican garbage tips, was rearranged with everyone sitting in neat rows, bowing to constant missives from the Editor, ordering that he did not wish to see any untidy desks. We now toiled away, alcohol free, in something like an insurance office, hunched at our terminals.

The Fourth Estate was now decaying, going gradually out of fashion and bankrupt. Over the years, I had become so cocooned that I was no longer able to compare my life with those of people outside the profession, people on average salaries who shop at M&S.

The comfort that came from the high salary no longer felt right; what I was doing? The way I was living wasn't about journalism. It wasn't the world of Orwell or even Patrick Leigh Fermor whose lives lived up to their imagination. In the theatre one night, I heard a character say, 'When you reach my age you realise that nothing has happened to you for twenty years,' and I felt alarmed.

'Everyone wants what we've got,' said Meryl Streep, in her film role as the cruel magazine editor Miranda Priestly in *The Devil Wears Prada*. But I wasn't sure any more. I had to find out whether I had another identity outside my paper: was I really a journalist at all or just a sociopath who had found a lucky niche in the 1980s when everyone was chasing the money with blades on their wheels?

The matter was resolved when I was sued by a liver-spotted actress, largely for mentioning in passing that she was ageing. The paper settled out of court and I went out of favour, a situation that can last from a week to a year, and it's best to accept it and keep your head down. I became discontented and obstreperous and suddenly I was unemployed, or freelance as we say. At least I was no longer stuck in a Faustian pact. I did not know then that there were no more Faustian pacts coming along. It seems that Faust only fancies you once.

I didn't get much freelance work, and I had no appetite for it, but I needed to do something as I was getting poorer. I had started my own accounts ledger. Across one page was written 'Increments'; across the other, 'Excrements'. As time ticked on, I realised I was in for a rather excremental time; no bright young woman with Lycra loins invited me into an office. I got some big pieces in, but I was never on a roll, there was no momentum, no sudden exciting sense of being wildly on my way.

On the bottom rung of the ladder again, providing diary stories on a freelance basis, feeding on scraps, I was more of a hack than ever before. I'd always wanted to paint and wondered about becoming an art teacher, so I went into teaching.

In mid-September 2006, I arrived as a teacher at HMP Wormwood Scrubs for the first time and stood in front of the massive castellated red-brick gatehouse with its rondel of Elizabeth Fry, the great prison reformer, looking down. The closed wooden gates belonged on the front of a fantasy medieval castle, and there didn't seem to be any knocker or bell. I stood there with my nose against the crack between them, trying to peer in until a man in a uniform waved me towards a humble staff entrance in what looked like an old public lavatory.

As I went in, a line was forming in front of another narrow entrance, of mainly young white women, faces creased and folded by nicotine. With their wizened faces, they could have been old news editors, except for the short skirts, bare legs, high heels and hooped earrings.

Little mixed-race girls in tight sexy pink skirts clung onto them, while their brothers swung upside down from the railings. All over the country similar straggling lines were forming. Over 165 children a year lose a parent to prison, more than in the days of Elizabeth Fry.

White SERCO vans, like giant refrigerators, with seven black windows, pulled in and out of the main gate carrying and delivering their never-ending cargo of offenders.

My straggling line of visitors moved slowly forwards. Once inside, on the left were boxes of vegetables and fruit, piles of letters to prisoners with colourful foreign stamps and a man who looked as if he might have just been released but, having nowhere to go, had slumped into the only chair in a narcotic trance. He was still there when I went home.

On the right of the entrance was a window for giving your name and department. On the wall beside it, a long list of things you can't take in: mobiles, laptops, alcohol, chewing gum, Blu-Tack, tin-openers, tools, porn, perfume, pyrotechnics, fire-crackers, cutlery and food stuffs.

A heavy metal door slid open and we were released into a kind of small pressure chamber. Once in there, although it is used by staff, not prisoners, there is no doubt you are entering a place of punishment. Its strange dinginess reminded me of a scene from a gritty crime film from the 1950s.

Behind a long row of dirty, scratched windows, warders – or officers as they now prefer to be called – toil away at what must be the most boring job in the prison: giving out keys and security passes and removing mobile phones. Behind them was a wooden sign like an old railway notice-board stating that 1,355 men were kept safely inside that day (the Scrubs was built to hold 860). Next to it a hand-written message declared daily orders of alert; apparently, that day, we were on 'high alert'.

If they were expecting a mass breakout or a riot, there was no sense of urgency; quite the opposite. We were in a tunnel where the normal atmosphere of everyday life had been replaced by something heavy and slowing, a feeling of torpor so strong that the sign could have been left from a distant, more exciting time, perhaps the Napoleonic Wars.

Eventually, another dirty-looking iron door ground open, and we faced what looked like a parade ground.

Beyond it, as far as I could see, more gates and man barriers of thick wire fences, the sort that used to contain monkeys in old-fashioned zoos. These were topped with spiralling, springing razor wire, medium and short barbed – impressive at first sight – but I discovered later that even this has to be carefully approved by Health and Safety so that it is not too lethal, with no bits sticking out causing danger to blind or careless people passing by or, perish the thought, trying to escape.

The slatted view through the grilles, which one man told me reminded him of a supermarket barcode, revealed another multi-storey cell block opposite across a square of grass, and making up the square was a sad-looking, squat grey chapel. The Victorian reformers who built the prison on the site of an old duelling ground made sure that every cell was carefully aligned to receive a weakened dose of either late morning or afternoon sunlight.

On either side of the path stood those earthbound piles called the wings. I was escorted along a cinder path beside one wing, through a slew of litter thrown down from the cells – food containers, old trainers, socks, oranges, crusts, sometimes whole loaves and toiletries. As we walked from above, I could hear laughter, shouts and Muslim prayers.

The Scrubs is a museum piece, and living inside it comes as a total shock to most men, who are not usually the museum-going type. I could hear youngsters screaming. Seasoned inmates call these noisy prisoners 'the kids'. Recently arrived, the unforgiving fortress-like walls, slapped over with green paint, brutally exclude them from their own familiar filthy streets, pubs, clubs and superstores, cut them off from the joys of Puma, Adidas and the wonders of the Argos catalogue, so they kick their doors, flick the ancient spy-hole flaps back and forth to create annoyance and howl in frustration.

When we finally reached the end of the path, a heavy main door was unlocked with three keys before we ascended a dark, dirty staircase to another heavy locked door which finally opened onto the Education Department. There was a new-looking notice above it, calling this the 'West London Campus'.

As I went through, I got my first smell of prison: carbolic, sweat, stale cigarettes and an unfamiliar sweetness, heroin – although I didn't recognise it then. After my long journey from the gate, I needed to use the loo, but there was only one cubicle, next to a shower, used by thirty-five women teachers and also women officers, coming off the wing – perhaps forty people or more. Male teachers fared slightly better having one cubicle and two urinals.

As I was about to go into the loo, a woman officer came in from a wing, through a barred gate nearby, walked in front of me and locked the toilet cubicle while she used the shower.

In the office, I asked one of the secretaries (now all called administrators), a young mixed-race girl appropriately named 'Jailah', if there was another loo somewhere? 'Over there,' she said, gesturing impatiently back towards the main gate, the way I'd come. Going back would mean being escorted through all those doors again, a hopeless idea.

Eventually the officer came out. She was tall with broad hips, wide calves and greasy hair scraped back into the kind of ponytail sometimes called the 'Essex facelift'.

'Isn't this the women teachers' toilet?' I asked, feeling rather bold as I had never met anyone like her before in my life.

'It's for the officers' use as well,' she said looking down at me beadily. 'This whole prison is for the officers' use.'

She wanted me to understand something before I went any further: I wasn't sure what it was, but it was something disagreeable.

When I did get to the loo, on the back of the lavatory door I read a notice saying bluntly, 'If you mess the pan, clean it.' With those uncompromising words I knew that I was in for the dirty handkerchief side of life that I had previously avoided.

'It's no good complainin', it's just the way it is,' said Comfort Golightly, slightly admonishing, slightly amused. She was a very large mixed-race woman, about forty, with a kind but slightly worried face and an Afro haircut that reminded me of Marsha Hunt.

'I have asked if we could have some special antiseptic spray to use in there on the seat,' she said, 'but they say there is no budget for it.' She sounded exasperated and sad.

Teachers obviously didn't make many demands on the prison. The staffroom was as dingy and dirty as the stairwell, with old changing-room lockers against the walls. It was crowded with rather dowdy-looking people who glanced at me through rheumy eyes which looked as if they'd been deprived of light for too long. Around a large table sat some black women eating homemade food out of plastic boxes. It looked heavy and smelled strongly of fish, and the smell of previous pescatorial lunches lingered in the air. A white male teacher passing by in cycling shorts and a helmet tut-tutted and muttered about the 'stink'.

The ladies took no notice and went on eating and setting the world to rights. I asked one of them, a tiny granny-ish-looking woman, what she was eating. 'Fufu,' she said, munching on. 'That's very popular in Africa isn't it?' I asked, interested, because I remembered the word from university, where I did a semester of 'African studies'.

'What do you mean, "Africa"?' she answered furiously. 'Africa is a very big place, a continent with lots of countries inside it.'

I had said the wrong thing. Africa to her was obviously some kind of raw wound which no white finger was allowed to touch. The other women stared straight through me.

'Why did I get such black looks?' I said to Comfort, who shrieked with laughter.

I was relieved that she laughed at me, realising uneasily that I probably didn't have the correct language to survive for long in the place. But there were people employed to put me right, including a 'diversity officer', rather like a strict Victorian parent or guardian to check that no one said or wrote 'the wrong thing'. I had entered a world where people were genuinely afraid to say the 'wrong' thing in case it caused grave offence. I felt forlorn for the loss of my newspaper world, where people make up headlines condemning Prince Harry for his gaffes whilst remaining themselves the most non-PC people in the world.

Brenda, a white woman in late middle age, with blonde flowing hair in the style of Brigitte Bardot, sat on the low staff chairs next to Jailah. They ate their sandwiches in silence. But Brenda was staring straight ahead as if she'd seen or heard something horrible, and I sensed it was me.

I was looking at a free newspaper, which had a piece about a survey showing that people who drink a lot of cola die ten years before people who don't. I suggested to Comfort that people who drink that much cola usually come from the lower social groups and die younger anyway. Without moving her head, Brenda swivelled two furious goggle eyes towards me.

'My daughter drinks loads of cola,' she said, leaving a long pause between each word, 'and she is not from the lower social groups.' Then, before I could disagree, she got up and stalked out of the room, and we never spoke again.

'It is probably best not to speak as if you are a social worker,' said Comfort.

To leave journalism for the public sector is to button your lip. I had made at least two enemies before I'd even met the men.

The first prisoner I saw was Groot, one of ten Dutch prisoners inside. He was the reverse of Brenda: old from the back, with long white hair like a character from *The Lord of the Rings,* but younger from the front, although his face was seamed by long drug abuse.

He moved slowly and silently about the staffroom, watering the stringy plant and washing mugs. Apparently he was a kind of 'tame' prisoner, the only one allowed in the staffroom. He was employed as a cleaner on 50p a day but was also given odd jobs to do for the teachers, including photocopying. As there were limited books in the prison and no access to the Internet, copying work was vital for teaching. But there was only one, very old photocopier, which often broke down. So if there was a queue to use it, or if you were busy queuing for the loo and didn't get your copying done before free flow, he would do it while you were teaching. He expected nothing in return, but the job gave him the chance to sit in the staffroom and read the newspapers when we were all out – perhaps a few moments of normal tranquillity.

On my first day, before I could start any teaching, I had to have 'Key Training'. Apparently we teachers were all vital cogs in the great machinery of prison security – even a failure to sign in in the morning might lead to 'a massive breach of security'.

Training took place in the administration block, home

of the other women's lavatory. It looked like a 1950s council block. To reach it, I had to retrace my steps to the gate. This meant finding someone with keys who had the time to take me there. Kantila, our Head of Education, agreed to do it. A Jamaican with big bouncing black ringlets, she had one of those purposeful management smiles that stop you in your tracks.

As we passed through the inner gate again, she glared at a lugubrious unshaven man working on the gate. He looked as if he'd been asleep but sprang to attention as we appeared. I was surprised he didn't salute as we sailed through. I was surprised to find out later that he was her husband and Jailah her daughter. She also had an aunt in administration and a sister in charge at another prison education department.

Key training was led by a neat little prison officer, middle-aged but fit and tanned, the sort who goes in for the Tour de France and always wears gym shoes. He took us through two hours of preparing for the worst and scared me witless.

Non-uniformed staff are the most vulnerable to hostage-taking, he said. Keep your eye fixed on the green alarm button on the classroom wall. Never go into a cell alone, and never let a prisoner get between you and the door. Just how was I going to manage that in the art room, a big place where we were all moving around?

His staccato voice created the image of the prison as a cross between a fortress and a Jesuit college, its inhabitants – mostly urban peasants from all over the world – were people you could never know or trust – a deeply hostile and suspicious place where spying was vital to security.

We were told to fill in security information reports (SIRs) if we ever overheard prisoners using words such as 'hostage', 'mobile', 'escape', – even 'Sim card'. We also had to fill in these SIRs on each other if we ever became worried about the behaviour of another teacher. The contents of the form were kept secret but would be acted on immediately.

It became clear that the overriding fear of the people in charge at the Scrubs was escape. Men in maths classes were not even officially allowed graph paper in case they used it to 'make plans'; however, as I found out, due to the very limited budget given to education, graph-paper exercise books were often all we had.

We were shown charts showing recent intelligence about escape plans. None of them had come to anything, but perhaps at the Scrubs they have never quite recovered from the sudden exit from D Wing, in October 1966, of Soviet spy George Blake. The ingenious Blake used a ladder made of knitting needles to scale a twenty-foot wall. He'd just been taken off the list of likely escapers, so there were red faces all round.

David Frost, in *The Frost Report* a year later, made a joke that the Governor had sent Christmas cards to all the inmates, wishing them the compliments of the season, 'wherever you are'. Cutting edge at the time, but since Blake there had been barely any bids for freedom – about one botched attempt a year. Just before I arrived, a prisoner had tried to escape from an ambulance taking him to hospital, but he'd quickly been recaptured.

In reality, very few people want to go over the wire or even walk out through the gate when they are obliged to go; the Department for Education and Skills figures for 2006 show that 61 per cent of offenders, about two-thirds, are reconvicted within two years; 73 per cent of offenders aged between eighteen and twenty-one return to prison at least twice; while the reoffending rate for teenagers aged between fifteen and eighteen is 82 per cent. The real problem of the Scrubs is that no one really wants to leave, at least not permanently.

Yet escape is still the biggest embarrassment possible for a governor. More than one might mean resignation. Suicides and murders do not count in the same way, perhaps because they are much more frequent and cannot be blamed on security.

After our lecture, I had to find out how to be a turnkey, surely one of the great historic jobs of all time. A few have been toffs who kept the likes of Elizabeth I and Mary Queen of Scots locked up, but mostly they have been the cold, unknown observers of history, pitilessly trailing a big hoop of keys around dark dank dungeons, opening doors or turning a blind eye for the right payment. Now apparently it is a highly skilled business, with a horrible amount of responsibility.

From the key-belt dangles a round old-fashioned key for opening cells, a Class I key for opening gates and a Class II for getting around inside.

When you go through the gates, unlocking as you go, you must not wait for people behind you to come through. Prisoners, it seems, have learned to call out, 'hold the gate,' to fool officers into thinking there is someone bona fide waiting to go through. Some lag, rash enough to want to leave, might slip past you.

Keys must be on the chain, and they must never leave the prison. If you take them out by mistake in your handbag at the end of the day, the police have to be informed, and God knows what happens to you, because if keys get into the wrong hands or get lost, it costs the prison about £3 million to replace them all.

After Key Training, you wait a few days, then apply for

the keys from Security who issue you with a black leather belt and pouch. Then each morning, you pick up keys from a pool left for each department. When you progress in the prison hierarchy you get 'designated keys', personal to you. I didn't like the idea of going to Security to ask for a key belt. The thought of that £3 million preyed on my mind – it was bad enough mislaying my own door key, so I decided to do without for a while.

When I was collected and escorted back to Education, Kantila's husband on the gate had been replaced by a small, wistful-looking white man smoking a pipe. He smiled and waved me through the way some guards do at border posts.

Back in Education, I tried to do some photocopying, but when I got to the machine I met Fatima, who was in charge of 'Skills for Life', a mysterious discipline I had never heard of. She was a good-looking Rastafarian, with a long, shiny, sculpted face below a broad elastic bandeau.

'Manners,' she said several times, staring intently at me. 'Pushing in, you think you can just push in, in front of me?' She nodded continually, and I felt vaguely scared. She seemed so angry, but there had been no sign of her when I reached the machine, and there was no paper being printed. But she certainly thought I had pushed in front of her, and it obviously infuriated her. Perhaps I had died and gone to a level of Hell where you are punished for all the pushing and shoving you did making your career hike in the 1980s.

'You've done it now if she thinks you've disrespected her,' whispered Comfort when I told her about it. 'Beware of the black sisterhood.'

She obviously wasn't in it herself but knew all about it. I had an uneasy feeling.

'They don't like anyone different from themselves,' she said as if speaking from long, painful experience, but she wouldn't say any more about it. She had her loyalties, but I was not sure where they were. I did notice in the first few weeks how black and white teachers in the main did not mix in the staffroom, apart from a few extroverts from both groups. The black women usually sat together round the big table, while other people, of all shades, tended to move quietly around them.

After what I'd heard in Key Training, I asked Comfort about the teaching. Was it so scary? Did you have to keep your back to the wall and your finger on the green button, as the trainer had said?

'It is very dangerous and we should all get personal alarms,' she said, 'but there is no budget for it. The worst thing is that no one tells us about the men we are teaching – they could be rapists and sex killers for all we know.'

So my first day as a teacher began. The Education Department, catering for about 120 men a week, was surprisingly small and cramped, with airless classrooms on either side of the wide corridor, bisected at both ends by heavy barred gates leading to the wings.

No one introduced me to my class, and after what I'd just heard at the training I felt very scared standing there alone in a room full of dangerous men. I hadn't felt so uneasy since I'd rented a room in a council flat in Lambeth and then discovered that it was in a high-risk area for muggings. How was I supposed to move about the room and keep my back to the door as the man had said? How was I supposed to move about and keep within distance of the alarm button? But the men didn't come near me, didn't speak to me, avoided all eye contact and disappeared into huddles behind screens they'd constructed by stretching bed sheets over easels and large painting boards.

From behind these wafted the distinct smell of spliffs

and roll-ups. They were not supposed to smoke at all, but how could I stop them? The smoke went into my eyes and stung my throat. Someone put loud reggae music on the radio. I felt as popular as an uninvited policeman at a private shebeen.

I couldn't see them or most of their work, which hung behind them in their tents. Some old paintings stood along the floor and could have belonged to former inmates for all I knew. The images I could see were relentlessly dark: blood, knives, huge teeth, faces drawn from what looked like Spiderman comics, plus a few soft-porn images of black girls in pink panties copied from magazines.

There were also paintings carefully copied from family photos, often showing small children in party clothes. One little girl sat in a metal swing, her little black face peering out from a hood like a pink flower. In the old-fashioned park swing she was surrounded by chains, and behind her stood a line of metal railings like prison bars.

Bill, aged about forty, very black and stocky, with a round face and long dreadlocks which looked like the contents of an old horsehair mattress, stood painting quietly in a corner. His images were quasi-religious, a black Madonna against a lurid orange sunset, Bob Marley with a halo. All his work was traced using an overhead projector. It seemed that no one drew from real objects or life, and their imaginations seemed to throw up almost identical images, like a line of graffiti tags.

Once there had once been four art rooms, offering pottery, printing and sculpture. On high shelves I could see the detritus of that golden age: portrait busts, papier-mâché masks, dusty ceramics and old portraits, including one by the painter Emma Sergeant who'd been teacher there for a while. Well, they were long gone, and something had happened to change all that. Now there was a feeling of deadness in the room.

After a few moments they surrounded me, demanding materials. I had been given one tiny set of keys to open a filing cabinet and a cupboard containing the register. The two main supply cupboards had to be unlocked by an officer, who was nowhere in sight.

'Miss, can I have some paper?'

'Miss, I need some pencils, have you got some pencils?'

'Miss, where is the drawing I did last week?'

'Miss, can you open the cupboard? We need to get the paint out.'

I struggled to open the filing cabinet. The keys didn't seem to work as they called out for pens, pencils, sketchbooks. It seemed that they'd never been given any equipment before, and I had no idea where to get anything for them. I had brought some pens with me, but I discovered to my dismay that I had left them behind, along with my water and a sandwich, in the wrong plastic bag, in the staffroom.

Panic made the register go fuzzy before my eyes. There were so many crossings-out, I just could not find where I was supposed to write. When I asked for names, they didn't reply.

Martin, a very good-looking Jamaican, just stared at me and said nothing, watching my distress impassively. He seemed to have a side-kick called Ben. A graceful lad with fine, almost girlish features and the unfortunately low-slung pants. Ben had a beautiful bottom, but I quickly loathed the sight of it and him, as he fiddled about, stretching, moaning and cursing.

All the time, men, not on the register, not supposed to be in the class, entered and disappeared into the shebeens or added to the scavenging crowd begging me for materials that I didn't have. When I asked them to leave, they ignored me and grouped around their particular friend in clusters. The only white men in the room were two small, pasty-faced twins called Atkins, who sat together at a table copying out letters for a 1970s-style poster. When I approached, they scowled up at me and covered the work with their skinny arms.

I knew that somewhere, beyond the art room and this nightmare, there was a qualified teacher called John, who was apparently in charge.

Much later, when I was getting used to things, when strangers asked if they could join the class, I would just say, 'that will be £450 down, and there is a two-year waiting list,' thinking of my own membership of the Groucho Club in Soho, where I'd spent so many languid hours. Jokes are currency in men's prisons. Even if they'd heard them before they appreciated them all the same.

But at first, my situation felt hopeless. Men poured in. If I excluded them, they returned a few moments later or, worse, they begged me to let them stay. If I asked men not to smoke, they ignored me or looked threatening and led mass walkouts, and at only ten past the hour on my first day the room was like an old-fashioned saloon bar. This, with P. Diddy on the radio, was giving me a headache.

Then I made the mistake of asking one of the Atkins twins to stop whistling as it was driving me crazy. He doubled up in a spasm of mock hilarity. I told him to leave the class. At that, all the men except Bill, rushed out of the room into the prisoners' loo at the end of the corridor, where not even officers seemed to go.

Bill went on painting as if nothing had happened. 'The art room is for chilling out,' he explained in a surprising

Welsh lilt. 'When you come here, you want to do your own thing.'

He was calm and kind, and I almost cried with gratitude. Thinking I could now do a spot of teaching, I took a proper look at his work: the religious, sub-Blakeian images, black angels, the people of Babylon. I wondered if he had ever heard of William Blake? He said he had, and I offered to bring in some books about the artist. He looked pleased but uncomfortably shy. I asked him a bit about his ideas, where did he get his themes, was he religious himself? He was evasive and then slunk off to the loo. Left alone in the room, I had a deep sinking sensation, but sometime later, thanks to Bill I think, the men returned in dribs and drabs.

Outside, Frank painted slowly on. 'Don't let them get you down, my dear,' he said. 'Things will settle down. Any chance you can get me some varnish?'

That first hour and a half ground slowly by, and then there was still the same amount of time to go. It felt like being abandoned in a quarry or dark pit. Then Bill stood across from me, putting both broad hands flatly on my desk. I noticed his long, vicious-looking nails, which must have made him lethal in a fight, a reminder of the dangerous world he inhabited beyond the art-room door.

'You will never get this class to work the way you want,' he said quietly but challengingly. 'Do you think you are going to come here and get people to start drawing and painting, everyone working away producing works of art? It will never happen. Every teacher who has come here has tried that, and it has never worked. They walk out of here with nothing.'

Speech over, he went off to his corner by the window, where his work was stacked up and carefully kept in folders.

Barno Nusrat appeared at last, smiling and calm, with a look that said, 'I know everything that goes on here, so don't worry yourself my dear.' I told him rather desperately that we needed more supplies.

'The men have been given all the materials they need,' he said, twinkling down at me. 'If they ask you for somethin', just say no or call me. They just want stuff to sell on the wings.'

I was surprised that fine paintbrushes and cheap India rubbers were wanted on the wings. 'Everything is for sale there,' he said, twinkling even more emphatically, 'there is a buyer for everything.'

When I looked into one of Bill's folders later, sure enough I saw that it was full of neatly stored paintbrushes and a box of pastels from the locked art cupboard.

By the end of the session, I retreated to the unlocked art cupboard. There were piles of magazines going back years and black and white books from In Tourist and other defunct Communist publishers. Some idealistic teacher must have brought them back from holidays behind the Iron Curtain. At last, it was free flow. Old Frank made another plea for some varnish, and the hostile strangers in my class trooped out to be searched and readmitted to the wings.

As they went, Bill hesitated. 'Don't go getting mixed up with the varnish thing,' he told me quietly. That is Simon's project. If you ask for varnish, he will get annoyed.' Bill obviously knew everything about the system, including the politics of the staffroom.

There were two other art teachers, both called Simon, but John, a tall young man with a long white throat and pale blue eyes, was in charge. He told me quite forcefully that he was applying for the job of Art Coordinator as he'd already been doing the job for six months. He seemed to think that I might be after it, obviously having no idea that I had no idea what an 'art coordinator' was and couldn't even manage the register.

He told me, when I asked, that the two Simons had apparently been there for years. I had no sense of them at all in the art room, as there was nothing in there to suggest there had been any input for years. I asked him, as inoffensively as I could, 'are there any plans for the art room?'

'I've got big plans for the future,' he said, 'I want to get a computer in there and start whole-class teaching, but in prison everything takes time and there is shedloads of paperwork.'

After my first morning, there was also a question I just had to ask Comfort: 'Why were there so many black men in prison?'

'They are black British,' she replied pointedly, looking as if she was on the edge of being offended.

The number of black prisoners in Britain's jails has risen 54 per cent – from 7,585 to 11,710 – since Labour came to power in 1997. At 16 per cent of those in gaol, the number of black prisoners is hugely disproportionate to the general population, where African and Caribbean people make up 2 per cent of the total. I was looking at the teeming core prison population, and men like Bill who were quite at ease inside, factoring prison into their lives the way other people plan to take out mortgages and holidays. But it clearly wasn't something Comfort wanted to talk about with me.

2

Throughout my years of drinking champagne, meeting celebrities and travelling everywhere by taxi, I had sometimes wondered about teaching. It seemed a civilised job and even a bit romantic – standing up there performing in front of a class of eager, receptive young minds.

'That is what people say if they've never done it,' said a teacher friend who'd been hard at it for twenty years. I thought his mistake had been to teach children or what are now known as kids. I was disqualified from teaching them as the Government now stipulates that you have to have Maths GCSE Grade C to teach in school – even cookery, art, needlework and PE. But I knew there was something called FE (further education) and that it was booming.

The Government was so keen on FE that they were using expensive advertising to extol the virtues of this 'lifelong learning'. There were television and newspaper ads and offers of 'financial incentives'. There were 'golden hellos' and 'key worker living loans'.

I associated FE with night school, where hard-grafting industrial workers went in for self-improvement and equipped themselves for better jobs. From when I first came to London I remembered evening classes, where creative middle-class people relaxed after work or as a break from looking after the children.

When I was a stranger in London, I had taken refuge in Morley College, at Waterloo, set up in 1880 to give penny lectures to the poor. It was a friendly place where you could attend classes for as little as 50p if you were signing on or a pensioner. Within its staid embrace you could keep warm, make friends, use the library and eat subsidised food. It was full of elderly women, their wide-fitting K Skips squeaking on the red tiled floors. They had a convivial time at cake icing, calligraphy and French, offering sympathetic advice to youngsters like me.

Although the Government wanted more teachers, it was surprisingly hard to get into teaching FE. To get on an initial teaching course, you had to have twenty hours of teaching going on – you had to have pupils, or students as they are now called, to teach, and I had no idea where to get them.

I rang the Department of Education and Skills to ask for advice. 'You are illegible,' said a young Asian Cockney voice. What did she mean I wondered, trying not to get annoyed. 'You are illegible wiv hout your howers,' she told me.

That was my first encounter with FE and its own special language, a strange half-literate tongue made up of overhearings and scraps of things not quite understood – rather like the language of Mary Norton's Borrowers, the tiny people who lived under the floorboards of a crumbling manor house.

I contacted Westminster University about teaching journalism. The girl I spoke to there, who sounded Afro-Caribbean, referred to it as 'West-minister'. Later, a young woman in their HR office sent me an email saying, 'We cannot employee you at this present time.'

I thought she'd made what in journalism is called 'a literal', a mistake you don't spot. But when I questioned it, the message came back again, assuring me that they could not 'employee me at the moment'.

I tried Newham College in East London, one of the biggest FE colleges in the country, which has had a £13 million investment in the past ten years and displays an impressive website. The woman in charge of the recruitment of teachers had a Muslim name starting with 'Begum'. I pictured her as a stout matriarch, a well-organised administrator.

But no, she was another young girl. Encouragingly, she said she'd get back to me the following Tuesday. That day came and went. After two days more, I phoned her.

'He 'asn't seen no CVs yet,' she told me, sounding irritated.

'You mean he hasn't seen any CVs yet?'

'He 'asn't seen none yet,' she said, more irritated. We could have gone on like that indefinitely as I was rapidly turning into a pedant before I'd even got near a classroom. Who 'He' was, she never explained.

I began to ring colleges and sixth-form colleges and write to private schools. I contacted a boarding school near Reading about teaching art to their sixth form after meeting Phoebe at a life-painting class. A well-bred sixth former, she told me blithely that the teachers at her school did all their A-level art work for them. She was at the painting class because she was just longing to do some painting herself.

'Parents pay a lot to send us to the school, so they like expect us all to get like A-starred A levels, so the teachers like have to do the work,' she explained.

Her school had no less than three art teachers, with one living in who also dealt with 'pastoral care'. It sounded great, like something from Mallory Towers, one of those schoolgirl novels. She said a teacher was leaving so there was obviously an opening, but I never received a reply.

Perhaps the fact that I had 'journalist' on my CV worried people, or maybe at fifty it was just too late to start another career and my time slot for employment had run out, thirteen years short of a pension.

Summer arrived, and all the places of education closed, except for the prisons, which never go on holiday. I rang up the Scrubs, and they said to come along. They didn't want a CV, just a willingness to be there, and I had to agree to do a teacher-training course.

Training began at a college in Notting Hill, which, by coincidence, had just won the lucrative contract to provide education in Wormwood Scrubs. It was they who had decided to call our cramped little education department the 'West London Campus'.

'Prison is the boom area for education,' said Jeff, our gentle Australian teacher. Perhaps I was going in the right direction; after twelve criminal-justice acts since 1997, the Government had just announced a new plan to build three 'Titan prisons', holding 10,500 more people, at a minimum cost of £1.2 billion.

There was also the fact that no other country in Europe locks up more of its population than we do. Between 1993 and 2007, prisoner numbers had risen from 41,600 to 80,100. A year later, that figure was up to 82,000. The London prisons were now the biggest schoolrooms in Europe.

I wasn't allowed to train as an art teacher, which is what I wanted, as it wasn't on the college curriculum – in fact, it didn't come anywhere on the syllabus. As a subject, art was nowhere. It obviously wasn't the sort of subject to which the Government was going to give any of its golden pennies. I had to be a 'literacy' teacher, which was really about teaching the English language at a low level, basically to non-English speakers. That was not what I wanted, but all the trainee teachers at the prison went to this college, and all your fees were paid. I had a continuous sense of confusion and unreality as I tried to morph from journalist into teacher and student, so I let it happen.

The first thing I noticed about this new identity was that it meant getting up very early. Newspaper offices didn't function till after 11 a.m., but now I had to be on the bus by 7 o'clock in the morning.

As I set out for my first college class, I noticed how London had changed. Travelling by taxi and company car, I had not noticed it before, now I felt like a stranger.

When I last took a bus, they were fairly small – about the size of a railway carriage. Most of the seats faced the same way, and you could hop on and off at will. There was even a conductor who often created a mood of entertainment, even when he was throwing people off, which could be quite arbitrary if he didn't like the look of you.

I still remember some of the conductors I'd known in my early days in Lambeth: Solzhenitsyn, with the grey beard nearly down to his ticket machine; the respectable Jamaican, the Belfast school mistress; the Rose West in big glasses who tried to force everyone upstairs. They all somehow looked like people who went to night school – at least, I could tell they led lives of great interest and intensity when they were not on the bus. On interesting routes into town, many conductors took on the role of impromptu guides to US tourists. Now they were all gone, and buses had become a bricolage of lurching metal where passengers sat in fours, almost nose to nose, knee to knee.

'Stop looking at me,' said a woman aggressively. I apologised nervously. I had glanced at her pink mohair coat. I didn't want to look at her face, but it was right in front of me, and the windows were so dirty that I didn't know where to put my eyes.

I was in a vehicle created by some kind of bus Beria, not interested in transport for the convenience of the public but in coercing his passengers into the 'right' sort of behaviour, which, in his twisted mind, meant forcing them to get embarrassingly close to strangers. Even the noise of the bell had changed from a reassuring bing into something like a strangled cry.

The passengers I had to face so closely had also changed. I faced women from the Horn of Africa, veiled women, white women with fat jutting out beneath their bras like truncated wings, the very old, the fighting drunk and the mad.

It felt as if I had moved abroad. On my first trip to college, I sat opposite a rough-looking man in jeans and old trainers. He looked Iraqi but spoke into his mobile in a broad Scots accent, discussing the result of one of his patient's MMR scans. I was impressed by him, but mostly I was irritated. I noted a strange new habit in mothers of putting their infants down on the seat next to them. On almost every journey I had to tell them to hold their offspring so that someone else could sit down. I once stood next to a Polish woman, who told me she was ninety. She looked it, but no one offered her a seat.

This feeling that I was now living in a strange new London continued when I got to my class. Of the twenty people applying to teach, only four were English and two Irish: the rest came from the Middle East and Eastern Europe. Some had been teaching in their own countries for fifteen and twenty years and now, at the same age as me, had decided to change country. Middle-aged people once settled down to enjoy their grandchildren, but now it seemed they had to get up and go, in some cases nearly 3,000 miles to get to work. Most of them had very poor English, including a Somali who told us in broken sentences that he had very little written English although he had already been a nurse in London for four years.

Their subjects were a surprise too – perhaps because I still think of education as being in some way academic. They wanted to teach 'nail technicians', hairdressers, childminders and make-up artists. We also had some esoteric students who taught kick-boxing and yoga. They too now needed a professional qualification to hold classes.

Standards cannot be assumed these days, and before we could start training as teachers we had to sit a basic literacy test. We were warned that on the final part of the course, leading to a Certificate in Education, there would be a maths test equivalent to Grade C at GCSE.

'Don't worry,' said a friend. 'You'll get that easily. It's all in modules, and you can take the test online, several times, until you pass.' I had avoided maths all my life, and now it was looming up at me again like a school bully I hadn't seen for years.

After the bad news about maths, we were told that our course, City & Guilds 7407 Teaching Certificate in FE, would probably be discontinued just as we reached the final third of it, to be replaced by a budding, flowering, blossoming set of acronyms: PTLLS ('Preparing to Teach in the Lifelong Learning Sector'), CTLLS (a Certificate in Teaching in the Lifelong Learning Sector) and DTLLS (a Diploma in Teaching in the Lifelong Learning Sector).

I didn't like change, and my course was changing before I'd even started. One of the administrators of the college, Mrs Breadcake, a smart woman in a Jaeger suit and expensive-looking beads, popped in to give us a little talk.

'FE is the adaptive layer of education,' she said, smiling assuringly the way professional people do when they've got bad news. 'We are not statutory like schools, we are not protected by charters like universities, so we can change all the time to meet societies' needs. We are truly agents of inclusion.'

I think this meant they were not protected from government meddling. Even the PGCE, a graduate certificate with international prestige, was probably going to be turned into something called an ACE. Worse, we were told we would also need extra courses after our course finally finished, to qualify for our QTLS (Qualified Teacher in Learning and Skills) status.

'This new measure means you are going to be qualified practitioners,' said Jeff, 'with the same educational status as doctors.'

He hoped to convince us that the changing of a word or a title would really mean a massive change of status. There was silence in response to this.

'Will we get the same pay?' I asked, and some of the class laughed. They obviously had more of a grasp of English than I thought. Mrs Breadcake gave me an inquisitive look.

As my first day in college went on, my spirits continued to sink. In FE, there are no kids, which is good – a bit like nursing without any really sick patients – but there are more rules and codes than in any fictional boarding school, and a whole new language.

'The role of a teacher as a mere purveyor of information is over,' said Jeff as if he had memorised passages from books. So much for the romantic idea of standing in front of an adoring class spouting beautiful words.

'These days, teachers are "facilitators," entering into a contract with the learner to help them fulfil their individual aspirations and needs. But the student must at all times own his or her own learning.'

I wasn't sure what this 'ownership' really meant but he seemed to be saying that you mustn't give or hand anything down to a student. As a teacher, you cannot put yourself into a superior position in any way. Your role as 'facilitator' might, if you are not watchful of yourself, involve the creation of a hierarchy with you at the top, something to be as avoided as racism.

'Your watchwords will be "inclusiveness," "accessibility" and "differentiation,"' said Jeff, sounding like an Evangelical preacher. 'Remember, IAD at all times.'

Inclusiveness sounds as if it means 'the more the merrier', but merriness has nothing to do with it. To get funding, a college must show that a large percentage of its students are disadvantaged or have severe learning problems, which brought us to the whole new language of disability.

In the classroom, we all had to get up and move into groups, 'workshopping' ideas on disability and how we would deal with this type of student in our class. A young Irish woman with long red hair told us she was interested in teaching people with dyslexia and dyspraxia. She described her knowledge of their special needs, which included specialised software and coloured paper, extra funding and resources, extra time in exams, about an hour before anyone else starts the paper. I quipped that I might become dyslexic myself if I ever had to sit a maths test.

'Are you seriously saying that eight-year-old children going in for an exam are lying?' she screamed out at me, with the kind of ire you once got in discussions about abortion, women's liberation and Bobby Sands.

'No, no, I'd never say anything like that,' I said. 'Of course not!' I sat feeling deflated, wondering what on earth had happened to the Irish. Didn't they used to be amusing, whimsical folk, always seeing the funny side if they could?

That was a racist notion that I would have to lose. Jeff warned us never, ever to fall into the sin of stereotyping or prejudice. To reinforce this, we were given a paper taken from a new schoolbook on citizenship, showing an old-fashioned cartoonist's view of the twelve nations of the EU. Each was a terrible stereotype: an Italian waving his arms, a Spaniard looking arrogant, a German lacking humour, an Irishman being drunk, an Englishman in country clothing walking a gun dog, which was a bit vague if it was intended to be detrimental.

The paper warned us that 'stereotypes lead to PREJU-DICE. Prejudice leads to hatred. Hatred leads to cruelty. The Holocaust is one example of this process in action.'

It seemed that the onus was on us as new, would-be teachers to put aside our genocidal impulses, if we could.

'Accessibility' means that entry to education is no longer judged by ability but by reference to an official quota for age, gender, ethnicity and background. Newham College promises a place to anyone who applies. So people with problems, perhaps previously seen as ineducable, will be let in. It also means that sixteen-year-olds who have been thrown out of school can also be accepted. 'You may even get them younger than that,' said Jeff darkly.

My idea that FE was not about kids was totally mistaken. It was a dumping ground for kids. There are now more kids in FE colleges than you can shake a stick at, if you were allowed to do such a thing, which you are not.

Differentiation is what used to be called 'mixed ability'. While in other areas of education this has been abandoned in favour of streaming, or 'setting' as it is now called, the FE teacher, and coincidentally the prison teacher, must demonstrate the ability to teach everything to everybody at the same time and to be sensitive to different 'learning styles', which are constantly being discovered, redefined and published by mainly Jewish American educationalists.

I got a glimpse of the future that day, and it showed teachers proving their commitment to IAD by having classes composed entirely of students with autism, aphasia, allergies, dysphasia, dyslexia, dyspraxia, echolalia, Irritable Bowel Syndrome (IBS), Obsessive Compulsive Disorder (OCD) and, perhaps, that lively newcomer, Restless Legs Syndrome (RLS). Let us not forget bipolarism, still known to some unreconstructed souls as manic depression. There is even 'unipolarism', which is the depression without the manic, which most people get – particularly teachers. Tourette's Syndrome, once extremely rare, now features on television game shows and is coming up alongside wheat intolerance as an increasingly popular complaint.

Language obviously has to be adjusted to keep up with all this. Jeff, in his gentle strine, warned us not to use the term 'brainstorm', as it might be offensive to epileptics. It is now preferable to say 'thought shower'.

In HMP Wormwood Scrubs, I had already heard the terms 'nutter', 'complete nutter', 'head-banger' and 'mentalist' freely applied, but I didn't bring that up as I was learning fast that in education it is better to say nothing to offend, and to enter education is to forget the reality of everyday life in favour of some ideal of right-thinking correct behaviour.

I was glad that prison, by its nature, had a particular reality, as solid as its walls: to teach these days, you need not only special coloured paper, myriad software, rails, ramps, lifts, pulleys and hearing loops. But in the Scrubs we didn't have any of those things and we had only one narrow lift, so that disabled people couldn't even get to the library.

I didn't mention this difference between life inside and the new world being created by FE outside, and during our day in college prison education wasn't mentioned at all. Despite all this theory about differentiation and inclusiveness, Jeff expressed no interest in it. When I mentioned it he had the same look of unease as when he talked about very young teenagers getting into FE – it scared or perhaps perplexed him.

At the mention of prison the other trainee teachers tittered. It was an embarrassment to them. 'You have classes in prison?' said the Somali, unable to believe his ears. 'Where I come from, people sit in their cells and they don't come out.' That was a view that most people seemed to have. 'West London Campus' or not, I could tell the Scrubs and the idea of prison education were going to be somewhat overlooked on the course.

3

My evenings were spent preparing classes for the following day, scouting through art books and videos of the *Teach Yourself Oil Painting, Fantastic Painting Tips, Try It Yourself* variety, hunting for dynamic ideas which might get the men going. I also had to start writing college assignments, in the new language of education with its Esperanto of acronyms.

At least twice a week I still covered parties in the West End for newspaper social diaries. I was careful to avoid the flowing champagne and luscious cocktails at these events, wrote the pieces when I got home and put them straight through, getting to bed late. Then I would lie awake or wake a few hours later, my bedside books and the cat's head illuminated by the phosphorous green light from my DAB radio dial. Listening to the *Navy Lark, Lord Peter Whimsy* and *The Goons*, I wondered about the next day behind bars: would the horrid twins be there in the morning to sneer at me as I fumbled with the cupboard keys; what would happen if Bill wasn't there to help; how could I reach him or the others and really try to get their work moving; would I be able to find Mr Nusrat to open the art cupboard; why was John so chilly with me?

During the day in prison I was terribly nice and polite, treating people with the kind of hesitant deference you use as a tourist in a foreign city. But this graciousness didn't seem to pay off much as most people were too busy to respond as they struggled with the photocopier or hunted for a free room to teach in. There were not enough rooms, and designated classrooms were sometimes taken over at short notice with permission from Kantila, causing tension between teachers. Often there were not enough chairs, exercise books or pens to go round. Bits of equipment such as tape recorders were removed overnight by Security.

A very good-looking black girl who taught maths took to staring at me, and, if I looked back, went on staring, as if she thought it would make me vanish. I felt annoyed, but she was a friend of Comfort, so I thought she must be all right. She and Comfort seemed to be in some sort of alliance against Fatima, who would charge in sometimes looking wildly happy, waving her large hands and giving 'big hugs', but at other times sat frowning to herself. Comfort picked me up on things I said but not in a hostile way, more as a form of engagement, and I realised that she was a bit of a loner, rather bored by the people around her. She enjoyed teaching me the new language of Education, which is mostly about what you don't say.

The administrators, apart from Brenda, were all attractive mixed-race girls with tiny heads and long legs in skinny jeans. They didn't seem to converse with older people, and if you spoke to them they replied in monosyllables or looked at the floor. I was surprised by how little they smiled. It was as if they were all perpetually sulking.

Some said it was tough on Jailah being the boss's daughter and that she had a baby at home. But the teachers were scared of her as she was rumoured to report people to her mother if they annoyed her. Her glum expression could easily become a furious pout.

It was said that Kantila adored her daughter, and I heard that aged seventeen, with no qualifications, she had once set up her own 'life skills' classes. Her mother only put a stop to it after indignant complaints from other teachers.

Some in the staffroom were obviously in their own world, fuelled by problems and quarrels going back years about which I knew nothing. One morning at the gate, I asked Marjorie, a small, dapper woman of mixed race, who had a strong Yorkshire accent, if she would escort me inside. She remained doggedly silent right across the yard, through the slew of detritus dropped from above onto our path. At one point, water came cascading down, and we both had to jump aside.

'That's a nice hat you are wearing,' I said desperately as we went up the stairs. She stopped and looked at me coldly. 'What business is my hat to you?' she said with such disdain that I felt shocked.

I followed her into the staffroom where I confronted her, saying, 'Please don't speak to me like that again.' She huffed and puffed and disappeared. I sat, feeling apprehensive, but none of the slumberers or the ladies sitting at the big table seemed to notice anything. They all had their own sensitivities and 'issues', as the modern cliché puts it.

I felt lost, stumbling along, not knowing who in the room I was crossing at any time but dependent on them for help, unlike my early days in journalism, when I had relied squarely on myself. Things were very different now. As a journalist I had always felt special; I had winged sandals and flameproof skin, always getting ahead, taking part in an ever exciting race, the goal of which was to see yourself emblazoned in print, but now I was just a teacher in a grubby staffroom that smelled bad. There seemed to be something doomed about the teacher's day, as if we never really got anywhere.

'Just keep your head down,' said Fran sagely. 'Be careful what you say and only say what people want to hear.'

She was Literacy Coordinator – my immediate boss. In her late fifties, dressed in a floaty floral skirt, cowboy boots and trendy denim top from one of the best charity shops in Notting Hill, she had once been a beautiful daydreaming hippy, living on a smallholding in Wales with goats and horses. Times changed, and she had adapted.

'I've done everything backwards,' she said. However late she'd left it, I could see that she was enviably employable as a teacher and administrator. Her only problem was to achieve what she could in the prison before being forced by ageism or sheer fatigue to admit defeat.

She showed me how to plan a scheme of work; she could even manage to cross-reference all the prison work with the National Curriculum. She could also make graphs, charts and boxes on the computer. This was about being a modern teacher – not a lover of poetry but a left-brained scientist of paperwork.

Fran also ran the prison magazine, *Free Time*, along with a radio-production course. She told me she had waited a year for a computer and another eight months after that for the software to arrive. She'd recently received three more computers so the men could do the magazine work more easily, but when they arrived, none of them had enough RAM to be any use. 'Bloody, fucking hopeless,' she said.

The teachers seemed to have to battle for basic resources, and with a £10 million cut in funding for prisoner education proposed by the Government for 2008, the situation didn't look likely to improve. It was depressing, but Fran had so much energy she made the task of teaching in prison seem viable.

'In prison, don't hope for anything,' she told me. 'If Security doesn't fuck you up, then the College will. The thing is to get round the system as best you can. It just takes a lot of patience.'

Morning classes lasted from 8.45 until 11.15 a.m., with a long, unpaid break until the afternoon session began at 1.45 p.m. or some days 2 p.m. The wait could be even longer if the officers, screws or mufti-men as they were called, chose to bring the men up an hour or so late, or perhaps not at all. Education was not a priority.

It seemed that my afternoons now had to be spent sitting in the staffroom avoiding certain people, getting stared at and trying to make conversation with people who really didn't want to speak to me because of race and class.

On my second morning in the prison, I had a visit from Mr Zippo, one of the heads of Security, a stout, furious-looking prison officer who always seems to be about to burst the silver buttons from his uniform as he swelled in indignation. He marched into the art room and asked me to step into the cupboard.

'Solvents, solvents, have you got any solvents in here?' he barked, jammed up against me, his popping eyes jabbing me up and down as if I had committed some heinous crime. I had no idea what he meant.

'You use them with oil paint,' he spluttered crossly, 'white spirit, turpentine—'

'Oh, no,' I said. 'We haven't got anything like that, but we could really do with some. How can I put in an order to get some?'

'You can't have any!' he shouted. 'They are banned. Men

use them to blind each other! They make bombs, and we've had napalm attacks! These are dangerous, terrible people. They have done filthy things!' And he stormed out, looking as if he hated me.

'Were you getting a telling-off?' said Isaac consolingly. He was a gentle youth, a mixture of black and Irish, in for drug offences and burglary. I said, 'Yes, for scaring the men too much and making them cry.'

Later, for a joke, I sometimes smiled at Mr Zippo, but he never smiled back and usually looked even more furious as if my very being represented a breach of security.

''E's got big problems with his women, dat man,' said Mr Nusrat in his most Caribbean accent, with his curious long smile.

'This morning Zippy had a go at me!' Comfort told me as we walked towards the inner gate soon after this incident. 'He shouted at me, "Get your keys out of your hand and put them on your key chain or else I'll take your keys off ya!!" I said, "I don't have a hearing problem," but I was shaking. There is still a mist in front of my eyes. All I can see is this blond gorilla with bulging blue eyes.'

Was Mr Zippo blond; did he have blue eyes? I had never noticed. His colour meant something to her, but, of course, I had never noticed it.

'What a bully,' I said. 'I don't know why he has to behave like that.'

'In Education, we don't understand Security,' she said, 'and they don't understand us. They would like to close down the Education Department if they could. They see it as a big nuisance and think it gives the men some kind of privilege. They never had education so they don't see why the men should get it.'

Some teachers took subversive action against Security.

Charley, who taught IT, whose father was a senior member of staff at the college, told me that a mysterious woman from Security visited his class every month to check all the computer files on the approved network, but she never looked at any individual computers and didn't seem to know that prisoners from Russia and the Middle East were particularly gifted at creating their own secret files. He also didn't tell her that although the USB ports on the front of all computers were sealed, there were four open at the back, unknown to Security.

'They don't know what they are afraid of,' he laughed. One up to him and the Russians. It was a good game, and he didn't intend to work in the prison for long.

By lunchtime I was usually desperate to get out into the fresh air. This was not easy as the prison seemed to have created its own microclimate, casting a pall of gloom and grime over the whole area of East Acton.

The local houses were not bad, a bit arts-and-crafty, but their 'For Sale' boards seemed to stay up for ever. They had the bleak look of the hard-to-sell. I wondered if perhaps I had the same look, but in the case of the houses it was due to location rather than age.

I roamed about for the first few days, visiting the Queen Charlotte's hospital café, a corner place with one woman doling out sandwiches and elaborate coffee to a long queue of hungry, irritable people. At the back of the hospital building, through dirty plastic vertical drapes, I found another café, a dark dive full of hospital porters. Some days I tried taking my sandwich onto the Scrubs itself, nearly 200 acres of grassland, trees and brush, right up against the prison walls. In the dying summer sun I lay down in long grass trying to relax, but the questions kept coming: what am I doing here; is this the right thing to be doing?

Towards the end of September, the weather was too cold for lying about and I discovered Hammersmith Hospital canteen. In the old days on Fleet Street I enjoyed lining up in subterranean canteens before an array of hot dishes served by large, bumptious ladies. Those bright steamy places had long been reduced to idiotic little bistros with chrome chairs, glass tables and microwaved pies. Hammersmith Hospital was something in between: traditional recipes poorly made. Cauliflower cheese with a white sauce made from water. Spotted Dick and apple crumble which were in fact American muffins in disguise, containing a sweetener, which tasted slightly bitter.

For the first few weeks in my new job, like someone stranded on a desert island, I remembered food I had once enjoyed: scallops with pea puree or perhaps a chilled fennel soup in Kensington Place with its great glass wall to the street allowing people going past to see the lucky diners inside. Not many people would want to stare in at us lunchers in Hammersmith Hospital, chewing on Halal goat stew and chilli con carne that had somehow been drained of all flavour. I was now living on the fat-drenched, flavourless side of London, where people ate what was put in front of them, without much question.

In those first weeks, most of my teaching hours were spent moving restlessly around the art room, from man to man, feeling useless: the twins always worked in the same letters in bright colours. I wondered if they would like to make some posters advertising the class. According to one of my new education books, this would involve their design skills and increase self-esteem as they would be doing something proactive for their group. The answer was no; they certainly would not like to do that at all.

They would sneer and grunt whenever I went near them,

lowering their tiny eyes, staring at the work protectively as if I was about to steal it. I realised this was about 'trust issues' but disliked them too much to want to build any bridges with them.

Good-looking Martin, whose head shone like polished ebony, spent each day copying, very, very slowly, in black paint, from a photo of Martin Luther King being arrested in Birmingham, Alabama.

'Wonderful', 'marvellous', 'most interesting', I said hopefully. No reply.

'Are you also interested in Coretta Scott King, by any chance? Do you know anything about her?' No reply.

Ben, with the lovely bottom, always close by, copied, very, very slowly, in black paint from a photo of Jimi Hendrix. He wouldn't say anything to me about his liking for Hendrix or why he had chosen this particular image, but he spoke to me occasionally, usually on the lines of 'You destroy the land, you steal everything from the black man.' Sometimes he made comments to the air as I went past. The words 'blad' and 'clat' would hang in the air, meaning either 'clot', as in blood, or 'cloth' as in sanitary towel – either way not friendly. But he was even-handed as he seemed to hate anyone who was not Jamaican, even blacks from other islands in the Caribbean and Africans, whom he accused of selling his brothers into slavery in the first place.

Before I'd gone to work in the prison, some of my friends had cast doubt on whether it was a good thing for a single woman to do.

'You will fall in love with them,' said one of my Afro-Caribbean friends. He detested the idea of prison and thought I shouldn't go there or take such a risk, and it had worried me a bit. I knew how charming black and Asian men could be, especially compared to reticent Englishmen.

But in the art room, seeing how they all stonewalled me, I felt quite safe from romance.

Among their dislikes, the black men also included Isaac. Being mixed race, he was not a 'brother'. They called him a him a 'coconut', meaning someone black on the outside but white inside. They also make jibes about his girlfriends, or lack of them, hinting that he might be gay, a hated 'battyboy'. Isaac just laughed at whatever they said. He was charming and light-hearted, although you could see heroin abuse in the premature lines in his face.

Perhaps their dislike also came from the fact that he was the only one who really painted expressively, as if he didn't care about the rest of the group. The men were not allowed oil paint, only thin, inflexible acrylic, which has no lustre and quickly goes grey if you put one layer over another. Despite this, Isaac struggled with it, constantly stretching torn bed sheets over easels and producing interesting abstracts in layers, scratching through shapes and letters, using his fingers, trying different methods to get interesting effects.

I brought him in a catalogue of work by Anselm Keifer, the great contemporary German artist who works by building up layers, using dust, dirt, straw, wood and detritus, to explore the deliberately buried past. Isaac was very interested, and it was such a relief to get a response that I felt like hugging him. But he was not tactile and I sensed that he was so fragile, or rather so hollow, that if I had squeezed him he would disappear into more art-room dust.

He was reading *The Kingdom of Fear,* by Hunter S. Thomson, and pointed out the line, 'You are a whole different person when you are scared.' I wondered uncomfortably if he knew how scared I was.

I left Isaac's bit of space reluctantly, at the same time realising that it was unwise and unfair to make any man into an ally. My feeling of isolation made me too crotchety with some men and too accommodating with others. The men were sharp, seasoned, and it was possible to get out of one's depth very quickly.

The little man at Key Training had seen them all as dangerous, almost like wild beasts that had to be kept at arm's length with a stick. That was not the case for me. They either hid themselves or were too friendly.

I remember pressing a little plastic tattoo transfer of a heart shape in diamonds onto one burly, black biceps belonging to a prisoner known as 'Moose'. A passing officer looked at me as if I was insane. I laughed and had a rather enjoyable reckless feeling, like being in school again.

Then I got a terribly stiff neck – not just a normal stiff neck: this one seemed to grip me in an iron vice, and I couldn't sleep at night. Moose massaged it, ignoring the no-touching rule. He seemed harmless, big and flabby, with dreadlocks like chewed Biltong sausages. He was good fun.

I drew his portrait and it came out well, although he had to sit still for over an hour. He wasn't officially in the art class, but he seemed to be a friend of Ben, and when they were together Ben lightened up a little with me. But then Moose started touching, grabbing, patting and playing a bit rough. He looked at me affectionately, but I felt there was something proprietorial about him.

At first, I treated this as a joke, as after all I had allowed it to happen. I was aware that it was my fault. He sometimes put a mobile-phone number on a bit of screwed-up paper on the desk for me and started pestering for mine. I ignored it. Mobiles were banned and it wasn't amusing anymore.

Then he put his hand on one of my breasts and I couldn't even pretend out of politeness or embarrassment to be amused. As I put my arm up to parry any more gropes, I could see that he was offended. He drew back, making a hissing, dissing noise through his bottom teeth. He slunk out of the room, and I knew that if anyone had seen it, or if he talked about it to Ben, I would be the talk of the wing. It was a little like being in a small village, except this one was patrolled by Security and full of listening ears.

I felt begrimed and worried. Ben and Moose might now join forces against me. Martin would be even more coldly contemptuous than he was, if that were possible. I had got myself into the kind of situation the college called 'a critical incident'.

It should never have arisen, and I didn't want to get him into trouble as I felt responsible. I kept quiet but went about dreading the sight of him. If he came into the room, I attempted to be distant but friendly, to make some hasty 'boundaries', trying not to make things even more unpleasant. He kept coming into the art room, mooching about without speaking much, sulking and aggrieved. I tried to go back to normal conversation, but when I saw the meanness in his face I started ignoring him.

'He holds people up at Shepherd's Bush with a knife and robs them of £20 notes,' Bill told me, and I had an unpleasant feeling that he knew everything.

I decided to tell Moose flatly not to come in to the art room anymore – he wasn't supposed to be there anyway. He appeared soon after, swaggering more than usual. John had made a rare appearance in the room and immediately asked him to leave. 'Someone has been pilfering,' he said, looking around accusingly.

Prisoners will usually obey male teachers, at least if they are young and strong-looking, but my unwanted guest sat down with his legs over the back of a chair and refused to leave. He started an argument with John, calling him 'a bitch and a woman.' I retreated but heard him say that I was 'scruffy' – true – but obviously, in his eyes, a terrible thing to say about a woman.

He still refused to leave. A guard was called and he was banned from Education. I knew I had had a narrow escape, I didn't even want to think about it.

Kantila looked him up on the office computer. We were never told what our students had done, and I felt it was better to be ignorant and unafraid rather than informed and unnerved.

I once heard Brenda, with the cola-swigging daughter, looking at the computer screen, suddenly announce, 'He's in here for sex.' No woman teacher wanted to hear that. Sometimes prisoners were marked as 'never to be left alone with women members of staff.' It was really better not to know, because there was nothing we could do.

On screen, it said that my man was a member of the notorious MDP (Murder Dem Pussies), one of nearly 200 active gangs in an area stretching from Shepherd's Bush all the way to leafy Richmond. This gang was responsible for a lot of low-level crime but was also connected to the death of a teenager called Kodjo Yenga.

Kantila said that he would not be coming up to Education again unless he slipped through accidentally at free flow. The thought scared me. She asked me whether I thought he might be dangerous to women, and if I had any worries about that I should fill in one of the confidential SIRs.

On the SIR form, I had to write out the details of the 'contact' I'd had with the prisoner. I gave a frank account of things and wrote that I thought he was potentially dangerous, he certainly made me feel very uneasy, but I felt guilty about doing it. By not keeping him at bay, I had made his life more difficult, but then again, he was a total opportunist and really in trouble for threatening behaviour towards John.

I took the form over to Security, who resided in the low brick council house inside the main gate. A woman with tiny staring eyes sat frowning at the front desk, the sort of character you might see in an old French detective film. Mr Zippo had a corner to himself, encased in glass. It was a very drab room, full of old coffee cups, cheap calendars without pictures and faded graphs.

I had to stand by the beady woman's desk as she read my report out loud. She then handed it over to a man on the other side of the room, and I had to go and stand by his desk, while he also read it out, in a braying Ulster accent. This was humiliating. I felt very exposed, but then they both lapsed into therapy speak, asking if I felt I had been 'damaged' by the experience, if I needed any help to 'get closure' and offering me the staff counselling service.

'I'm fine,' I said nonchalantly, and they looked disappointed. I felt they wanted some excitement and some way to show that their power extended over all matters in prison, even the pastoral. I savoured a toxic mix of prurience and political correctness in the air and felt like saying, 'If a woman my age can't cope with a man feeling her up without going nuts or feeling "damaged," it really is a bit sad.'

When I said this to my colleagues later, they seemed to find it amusing, as if a bit of common sense was somehow radical and laughably old-fashioned. I was becoming a bit of a 'hoot'.

Teachers were supposed to keep a 'personal development diary' and write down all such incidents. It had been a 'learning experience', I couldn't deny that, and I resolved to make proper boundaries with the men in the future.

At the same time, I carried on trying to improve my 'inclusiveness' in the classroom. In one corner of the room near the sinks were the tents containing the black clique, but round the edges of the room elderly Asian men – inside mainly for insurance fraud and incest – sat quietly working away at their own projects. Fatalistic, polite, rather withdrawn, they carefully copied out photos of gentle landscapes with the cheap coloured pencils provided. Their marks were usually so faint you could hardly see anything on the paper.

In another corner sat Mr Massoud, a middle-aged Iranian who smiled all the time and never spoke to anyone in the room. He copied richly decorative paintings by Matisse and Renoir, relishing the colours. 'I want to make beautiful paintings about love,' he said. Occasionally, he received visits from Tariq, an Iranian friend, who also had a fixed defensive smile. He would take my hands between his and bow low over them, as if he was overwhelmingly glad to see me, a lily in the desert. He desperately wanted me to paint a copy of a photo of him and his girlfriend sitting together in a garden. To me she looked like an uneasy, fat English girl he'd only just met. The body language was all wrong. But he kept saying that she was 'so beautiful', he loved her and would marry her in prison. If I made the painting, he said, I could come to their wedding.

Tariq also liked to show photographs of himself with famous people, at least famous to him: the Prime Minister of Iran, the Iranian Ambassador to Turkey, an embassy official from Syria. All the images showed him at the forefront of the picture, with glassy eyes and that same fixed smile. The important men around him often seemed to be watching him out of the corner of their eyes, politely concealing their surprise.

The men ignored these photos and tried to ignore him, but Mr Nusrat was fascinated.

'He must be a really important geezer,' he said, looking very impressed. Shortly after, as I was coming out of the art-room cupboard onto the corridor, I saw him pushing a packet of tobacco into Tariq's hand, which was curved up behind his back. Dealing went on all the time, which I found a conundrum, as Security dominated our lives.

My main worry was that I still had no idea how to get the men to let me teach them. One day, Raj, a Sikh youth who'd drifted in from another class, said he wanted 'to learn to draw'. At last someone who needed my services. But before he could join art, he had to get permission to leave his other class and to pass the right level of maths and English. After two weeks of negotiation, he made it into art, but when I put together a still life from the bits and pieces on the shelves and unlocked some charcoal, he wouldn't tackle it.

'I can't use charcoal, Miss,' he said, 'because we only get a change of clothes once a week.'

A good point, as they were given no overalls for art. Other men refused to use charcoal or paint because of this problem, especially if they were expecting a visit from outside and needed to be smart.

They were always short of clean clothes. Some men managed to swap things to get a couple of extra shirts, which they wash with overpriced detergent, paid for out of their basic £11.90 weekly pocket money and dry overnight on the hot pipes in their cells, but most just tried to guard themselves against getting dirty in the first place.

But the main reason they didn't like charcoal was that it was messy on the page, not easy to control and encouraged much wilder drawing. They liked hard, sharp pencils, which were easier to control, although they were difficult to get as we were not allowed anything to sharpen them. Better still, they wanted stencil sets so they didn't have to make their own lines at all. None of the men wanted to make quick sketches or draw or paint anything that wasn't printed in a book.

For them, art was about status, and no one in the room apart from Isaac, who had no status, would risk failure. 'That's shit, man,' someone would sneer, and that would be the end of that attempt at drawing. None of them had heard the modern shibboleth that the process is just as important as the end product. I said it often but could not get it into their heads. They had no concept of creative failure.

I thought about all those pampered middle-class infants whose mothers put their work up on the kitchen wall, how they grow up steeped in the idea that they are free to experiment, that self-expression will bring praise regardless of success.

I couldn't imagine how these boys had lived, what their mothers' kitchen walls were like, but now they all craved something slick, glossy, sentimental and highly finished, something neat to show Mum, the baby-mother and even the probation officer.

One afternoon, our torpor was broken when three stout American women missionaries, silver crosses dangling, appeared all the way from New Jersey to see us. They pottered round the room and looked terribly pleased with everything and everyone. Bill came to my aid again, turning the radio down, smiling and chatting to them. Puffing out his muscular chest and standing up straight, he looked as if he were on parade.

Their genuine inclusiveness was very touching, but it was a bit worrying when they said they had seen nothing like our art room in any of the prisons in New Jersey. What sort of prisons do they have over there if they thought our gloomy hole was so fine? Perhaps they were just impressed at the sight of so many fierce black men working away so industriously. I was impressed myself, but it was a blip: as soon as the matrons had gone a fight broke out after someone stole tobacco from Martin. An officer put his head round the door for a few moments, and then they all ran headlong into the loo for sanctuary.

As I was sitting there alone, looking at an art book, a very smart-looking black woman in a tight black suit, sporting elaborate oiled ringlets just like Kantila's, appeared in the doorway, followed by several smiling attendants. This was Loella, who ran the Education Department before Kantila and wanted it back.

I was told later that whenever Kantila flew home to the West Indies, which she did in three- to four-week chunks, Loella returned and rushed round making notes on everything, trying to find fault with how the department was being run.

She then made clandestine reports to the College. She eyed my empty room. Even Isaac had gone off somewhere. 'They'll be back in a minute,' I said weakly. 'They sometimes need a loo break.'

'I think you need a little more support here,' she said, with a gleaming smile that said, 'this is a piece of luck, lack of supervision, total chaos.'

In one stride, she crossed the corridor, kicked open the door of the men's lavatory, a place not even officers would venture, screamed at them to get out at once or she would have them all permanently banned from Education.

They all trooped back quiet as lambs.

'You shouldn't have been left alone with a class like this,' she said with a gleaming smile of satisfaction and disappeared. I heard from Fran that Loella wrote a critical report about Kantila's management skills and sent it off to Glenda Gittings, who was in charge of the prison contract at the college. In the meantime, Fran wrote a letter on behalf of Kantila, accusing Loella of undermining the department. Kantila claimed to have a degree in business studies, but Fran said she had left before she finished it and was 'not good at letters.'

Kantila never said anything to me about the incident and never asked me how I was getting on in the art room. She gave me a feeling like the beginnings of a slight cold, something unpleasant that might flare up but might also hopefully die down.

To try to get on her good side, I thought I might use some of my journalistic contacts for the benefit of the prisoners. I suggested asking Tony Benn, the former Labour minister and raconteur, to come in and talk to them about his life in politics, his meeting with Nelson Mandela, his views on the importance of prisoners getting the vote and becoming politically involved.

Fran was enthusiastic. Kantila gave the OK, and I contacted Mr Benn, who agreed to come in when he had a free afternoon the following month. In the meantime, I carried on trying to find a way to get the men to explore their creativity rather than idly repeating themselves like bored children with colouring books. There had to be a way. Differentiation: wasn't that supposed to be about finding something to suit everyone – or was that inclusiveness? And what about the much vaunted 'learning styles'? I wrote an essay about them but really had no idea who in the class had what, as I was a long way from getting enough response to find out.

Educational theory was new to me, and it struck my brain like a new language. Every lesson plan had to have an 'objective' and an 'aim'. One of these was long term, one short term, but I kept getting them mixed up. I roughly decided my 'objective', short or long, was to give them some basic skills, an awareness of basic measuring, line, tone, proportion and perspective. But how? I tried to tell John how hard I found it being in that horrible room and getting no response from most of the men.

'Yeah, yeah, there is a problem,' he'd said, gazing into the middle distance. Not long after, he got his job as Art Coordinator and seemed slightly friendlier, but as for his plans, there was no sign of any change, and he spent most of his time in the staffroom doing paperwork and looking at the office computer.

He decided to order more equipment, including new chairs and to organise an art teacher's meeting once a month, so at last I was to meet the other teachers. The Simons were middle-aged – one was edgy with a striped vest, goatee beard and an earring, the other very quiet, not even greeting us when he arrived.

John told us that Quiet Simon was planning to start a portrait course and also wanted to get a computer in so the men could do some 'digitalised work'. There has been no portraiture up to then, apart from the sketches I had been doing. I fancied running a portrait class myself, but kept quiet about it.

I said I would like to change a few things, perhaps do some whole-class teaching so that I could really do some old-fashioned input stuff, but the Simons took on that vaguely distracted look that people wear to indicate that they've heard it all before and can't wait for you to stop.

'There are very old prison laws and traditions here,' Edgy

Simon told me flatly. 'Ancient ways that must be respected. The men have been doing things in the same way for generations; no one can come here and just expect things to be the way they are on the outside.'

He created an image of prison as a world of fables, traditions and codes, where men scratch on the walls, tap on pipes and make artefacts out of bits of matchwood and coiled string. As far as I could see, the art room was used entirely for 'chilling out' as Bill had put it, and no one wanted things any other way. Certainly no interfering woman was going to change it. I felt as if they saw me as a Margaret Thatcher figure.

Edgy Simon also said he was planning to 'bring in' black artists to talk to the men and demonstrate their work. Where was he going to get them from?, I wondered. I knew a lot of artists but hardly any were black – perhaps he meant Chris Ofili. But this was a test, I knew, a crude posture to show me his political position and to find out on which side I was.

I let him confirm his prejudice against me by saying that art should not be based on race. John cut in and gave a kind of generalised reprimand about people 'wasting paper and teachers leaving the cabinet drawers unlocked'.

Someone, naming no names, had left one of the drawers to the filing cabinet open after a class, and a huge haul of stuff had been nicked. 'They are giving it out on the wings right now,' said John, looking very pained.

There was a silence at this news, and for a moment all eyes were on me. Then by some chance my cowed, befuddled brain threw up the fact that I had been collecting my security pass that particular morning, so it couldn't have been me. The subject was quickly dropped and we passed on to other matters: Edgy Simon was planning a course on black history to tie in with 'Black History Month'. There were already pictures of Mary Seacole everywhere, the great rival to pit against the all-white Florence Nightingale.

As the meeting ended, Simon caught sight of a tabloid newspaper sticking out from my many plastic bags. 'Read that a lot do you?' he said with a contemptuous little smile. I smiled back and didn't let on that I was actually working for it that very night.

At 6 p.m., I slung on my cream Catherine Walker dress, which was holding up well with only a few spills down the front, slipped on my increasingly battered Jimmy Choos and headed off to the National Portrait Gallery for the launch of a glossy new book by Tracey Emin. On the stage above us, Madam sat, ankles crossed, head cocked, coy as a cockatiel, interviewed by the Director of the Gallery. I didn't write down anything she said as there were no good quotes. She went in for faintly disputatious flirting like a child talking to her indulgent father, as if her clock had stopped at the age of three. But she was undoubtedly one of those lucky people who knew exactly what she wanted and just went for it.

I headed to the Criterion Theatre for the opening of a new production of *The 39 Steps,* then on to the opening party at the Café Royal.

The newspaper told me that there was a chance that Kate Moss might show up, so I had to be on full alert. The foyer of the café was thickly jammed with photographers. Some of them got inside and were pushing and jostling to get down onto the dingy well of the dance floor. They didn't need to work so hard as there was no sign of Kate.

I made my way laboriously around the cast of a TV sit-com about a group of sexy thirty-something flat-sharers which was very popular in the early 1990s. They were all still good-looking but a bit jaded now, and none of them seemed to be speaking to each other. Only two of them had 'made it big', by getting into films. A bit of a melancholy do, but Kate missed a lot of champagne and some good canapés.

On the way home, standing at the bus stop like Cinderella back in her rags, I saw an elderly white man deliberately crash himself into a Chinese girl standing near me. She was very upset, crying with shock and anger. I tried to comfort her, saying, 'He was drunk, he was crazy.' A Middle Eastern man nearby burst out laughing as if it were the most entertaining thing he'd seen in ages.

'What's so funny?' I snapped in my new prison voice, and he shut up immediately. How I detested his stupid face and his response, springing as it did from his lack of any frame of reference for what he could see around him.

In my journalism I had to get stories, and I had to meet deadlines, and I always managed it, but in prison I lived in confusion, always on the edge of panic. To make things worse, I saw, in the distance, a mountain of paperwork steadily approaching. Apart from registers which kept changing every day as men came and went, prisoners had individual learning plans to keep up plus personal-development plans. We also had to write down class numbers and reasons for absences, even if we didn't know them.

I also had to work on my weekly assignments. For my first one, I had to find a method of 'assessing learners' needs' – not easy when hardly anyone would talk to me.

One of my fat education textbooks said this assessment had to include their 'abilities, aspirations, motivation, (extrinsic and intrinsic) existing knowledge, individual learning styles, cultural background and life skills.' I decided that none of my students had any of those, apart from a 'cultural background', which they wouldn't or couldn't discuss. To make an assessment, we were supposed to write out a formal questionnaire asking the students to provide details of their age, background, previous qualifications and aspirations, also such things as what sort of art they liked, favourite painters or sculptors. I knew with a sinking feeling that I would get no replies to any such questions, except from Isaac and Old Frank.

My fellow trainee teachers, the nail technicians and kick-boxers, probably had students who would tell them all about their backgrounds and learning needs, but I didn't. I found out later that they had different problems: their students were perpetually late, absent or turned up full of lager or worse. One class I heard about was dominated by a heroin addict. At least in prison you avoided all that hassle; they wanted to be in the classroom, even if they refused to listen to a word you said and only wanted to do their own thing.

In my first 1,500-word essay, I trotted out a lot of what I knew I was supposed to say, embracing new words such as 'summative' and 'diagnostic': 'Assessment can be diagnostic, by means of which development needs may be identified; formative, in its potential to provide feedback about progress and standards; and summative, making possible valid and reliable judgements about competence.' My mind closed down after that, and my essay turned into a long shriek about the problems I was facing trying to make assessments in a prison environment:

'Teaching in prison involves special sensitivities,' I wrote, disingenuously quoting Edgy Simon: 'There is an ancient prison culture going back to the Napoleonic Wars or even earlier, which excludes and mistrusts all authority figures, including teachers. The Scrubs is mainly a remand prison with men there for a short time, unable to immerse themselves deeply in a course of study, uncertain of their immediate future. Any action will be mitigated by the needs of the prison. Men are constantly called out of class, having to attend doctors' appointments or meet probation officers, etc.'

I decided to show them some videos as a way of assessing them. This might also create a little collective interest and reveal some 'group dynamics', always a buzz phrase.

The prison had no film resources, so I had a look in the college library. After showing my passport, national-insurance number and a utility bill to get a library card, I found they didn't have any art videos and very few art books. I came away with an old BBC 2 documentary that they were about to throw out, about Matisse in Morocco, showing beautiful scenes from North Africa.

That night, I wrote in my first lying essay: 'Four men [in fact only Isaac and Massoud], from a group of eight, said they would be receptive to workshops about art history as they are interested in the work of Matisse. [Only Massoud had heard of him.] Other men in the class want to be left alone to copy out of magazines, but all needs have to be accommodated. Many men have limited education and short attention spans, but all of them need to be challenged to develop.'

I thought that once they were used to doing something as a group, such as watching a video and discussing it, they might manage a group criticism, each man presenting his own work for the group as a whole. This would encourage communication skills and lower defensiveness. I was sleepless with worry, listening to Jimmy Clitheroe and Lord Peter Whimsy into the early hours.

Mr Nusrat found me a free television and put the film on, but it was a bit difficult to see, with flickering patchy film and strange longueurs in the dialogue between Matisse and the interviewer. Morocco looked beautiful but rather faint. It didn't matter, as I was the only person who watched it. Even Massoud didn't come to the class as he explained he 'just wanted to get on with his own painting'. Most of the men went outside to smoke.

Isaac said he was listening from a distance. 'Well, I hope you found it interesting from over there,' I said, trying not to sound bitter.

'Yes, very,' he said, remaining on the other side of the room.

'Why was it interesting?' said Bill, suddenly scathing, the full philistine, resentful of high culture. I was too pissed off with him to reply.

'Most women art teachers don't stay long,' said Isaac unhelpfully. 'The last one was found crying in the cupboard.'

Fran suggested I should try the 1996 film about Basquiat, the successful black American graffiti artist. I didn't know his work and resisted the idea, thinking about Edgy Simon with his right-on ideas.

'Most of the men won't watch films about white artists,' said Fran bluntly. We put it on in a separate room usually used for music, so that the men could go on with their own work without feeling pressured into doing anything different. At first, only Isaac and some outsiders came in to see it, and they all said they'd seen it before as it had been on television late one night. Bill slid in and sat at the back for the last fifteen minutes. I gave him a smile of gratitude, like a woman who thought she'd been stood up but discovers her date is still on.

We chatted later about likes and dislikes, and he admitted that the highlight of his week was watching *The Antiques*

Roadshow. He had the dream of one day opening a small antiques business back in Cardiff.

He always helped me, remaining cool, unobtrusive, never creepy. One day I was helping a burly young black youth who wanted to copy a photograph of one of his children. I was trying to get him to make a wider range of tones and to mix colours himself rather than just pouring colour straight out of the container. Earlier, Mr Nusrat had spoken to him, and they'd both been aggressive.

'Bitch,' he said to me, 'you ruined my picture,' biting his lip and clenching his fists. I stepped back, and Bill leaned across and I heard him say very quietly but firmly, 'Back off, man, you are scaring the lady.'

Near the end of the session, the student, probably afraid of being banned, apologised to me, and unsure what I should do for the best I let it go. But I felt he was dangerously volatile and I was terribly vulnerable.

In bed at night I had fantasies about being in a hostage situation in the prison as described at Key Training, but I was always rescued at the last minute by Bill. I could not do without him.

I knew I was wildly lacking experience compared to someone like Fran. Tariq came in all the time with his celebrity photos. The men in my class began to resent him. He kept asking me to paint pictures and offering to pay people to write letters and print them out addressed on his behalf to his girlfriend. I didn't know how to stop him, but when he went into Fran's class and annoyed her men, she accused him of 'bullying' and simply had him removed from Education.

Brenda looked him up on her computer and discovered that he was inside for rape. I wondered if his victim was the glum-looking girl in the garden.

I became very anxious. Perhaps I have an exaggerated work ethic, but because I was in a new job and a sessional worker paid by the hour, I did not want to take any time off. If I stopped, I might not get going again, and I also had the college classes to attend and did not want to fall behind with the assignments. I later discovered that some student teachers never did them, or saved them all up until the Christmas holiday or after the course had officially finished. The deadline for finishing the course could be extended almost indefinitely, but I dreaded getting behind with things.

I wanted control over things in this strange new life I was leading, but the stress of it made me feel battered and weak. After a month inside, I started itching in one ear, followed by a feeling of congestion, then a grinding pain. I realised, with a bit of a shock, that no longer a staff journalist with company medical insurance, I would have to use the NHS, along with all the people who shop in M&S and read the paper I once helped to write.

To see a doctor I used to travel from my desk up to the fifth floor of our office, where various jaded locums were always available. Now I couldn't even get an appointment. My local GP only gave out appointments if you rang at 8.30 a.m. or 3 p.m. Everyone rang at the same time but I didn't even get to join in that scrum as I was at work at both those times. To make sure of getting an appointment I had to go to the surgery personally, missing a morning or possibly a day's work, so I joined in what was to me the new custom, once only used by people who'd been struck off their doctor's list, of going straight to a hospital A&E department and waiting there for two hours in the break between classes.

The following day, hardly able to hear and feeling dizzy, things seemed unusually chaotic, and I realised that to cope with prison you needed to be fit. John appeared suddenly and told us, almost as if it were nothing, that he'd just been on the wing and had seen a prison officer punched unconscious. It had happened over some small issue. A prisoner attacked the man so fast that he didn't have time to press his alarm. Some inmates jumped on the attacker to try to stop him, while other men dragged the officer away to safety and called for help.

A discussion started in the art room, and most of the men said they would not have gone to the aid of the prison officer. Some said this for racial reasons but also out of bravado. I felt afraid.

John seemed unperturbed, his pale blue eyes as calm as ever. He was almost merry, as if he'd seen something exciting, but I wondered what I would do if I saw something like that. Would I ever recover from seeing such savage violence? I didn't feel well enough to deal with it.

I was struggling and didn't feel valued by anyone. Shortly after I returned after my ear problem, Fran told me that the Governor wanted to know exactly why Tony Benn wanted to visit the prison. He thought that Benn must have a particular motive. I sent back a memo saying it was for educational purposes, citing Benn's meetings with Gandhi, Mandela, etc. Also, I thought that the old politician had ideas about encouraging prisoners to vote. As I sent this I had an ominous feeling and I wasn't surprised when Fran said it was a 'No' to that one. I didn't feel that the Governor had any interest in anything except security.

The hard core of hard men in the art room remained uncommunicative, refusing to learn anything from a white woman. They had never had anything to do with people like me in the past, and they didn't intend to start. Their attitude, the difference between them and me, brought back memories of my first inner-city summer, pungent with racial tension and dog-shit baking in the sun.

In 1981, I was still in a frenzy of excitement at being in London, the unknown place where I had been born. I'd left London when I was adopted at six weeks of age and taken to a new home in the Midlands. At twenty-five, I was back, exactly where I wanted to be. I couldn't understand why anyone would live anywhere else, but at that time I felt that I still hadn't really found the London I wanted so badly.

I could not believe that this Lambeth was London, because it was so depressing, so alien and frightening. Where were the people who once did the Lambeth Walk? Forced to do the Lambeth Sprint to the Nearest Taxi Rank or the Lambeth Hide Indoors Behind a Steel Grille.

The fear of street violence I had as a newcomer nearly ruined my days, as people old and young were constantly being mugged and the threat of attack seemed to be hanging in the air like the filthy plastic bags caught up in the dying trees.

I was at the Oval House theatre club one evening – Tim Roth was one of the young wannabees there – and a young black actor stood up and said, 'It's going to be a long hot summer, brothers.' The next day came the Brixton riots.

A few years before, as a student, I would have applauded this as an episode in the 'class war'. I was still very much a radical as I stood on the pavements in Brixton watching bricks flying into the air, terrified old people – black and white – distressed and crying while gangs of black youths ran in formation up the centre of the street then split into small groups as they looted shops. I heard that their overall plan was to 'reclaim' the decaying streets for themselves, for their own kind. I didn't admit it to myself for a long time, but I didn't like what I saw of the revolution.

I found work as an auxiliary nurse for St Thomas's Hospital, working on the district, as we used to say, as a 'bath attendant', visiting people in their homes and doing six baths a morning. I began walking miles over the broken pavements of Lambeth in squeaky plastic shoes, into housing estates, where I met old white ladies, the last of the original Lambeth Walkers. It was clear that they were living, ignored and trapped, inside the disputed 'no go' zone created between the black youths and the police.

That's the way it was, and if you didn't like it you kept quiet. Even then, being called a racist was the equivalent of being called a witch or a Jew in previous ages. After being mugged for the second time, a young neighbour upstairs suggested that I might be guilty of 'racist body language' which was inflaming my attackers. After that, I did the only thing you could do to escape: I got rich and moved over the river. I got a job on the national paper where I never saw another black face for fifteen years.

I'd spent almost twenty years avoiding multiracialism or, rather, like most successful people, I rarely had to see it, unless I chose to visit the Notting Hill Carnival for an afternoon, which I didn't, or had a curry in Brick Lane. Now, in the art room, I was back staring into black faces, impenetrable as Bambara masks, with the same vacant but resentful eyes.

'You hate music,' said one of the twins to me one day, as Notorious Whoever throbbed and raged on, beating me like a cosh. He spat the words out as if it was the most shameful thing he could possibly say about me.

I did like music, but it was true I didn't like their music, or their obsession with it.

The situation with the twins seemed irredeemable, but then one of them was bundled off to Belmarsh and his brother immediately becomes less vindictive. If I approached, he kept his head bent over his work, very sad, almost silent now that his brother had gone.

Two new prisoners arrived: Vere, a black Londoner charged with being in possession of drugs and keeping prostitutes, and Rupert, a white middle-class man, formerly employed by Barclays Bank, now a little down on his luck.

4

Vere wore his own clothes as a remand prisoner, and he looked striking in an expensive black leather jacket, crisp white vest, tight jeans and lizard-skin shoes. In his early forties, sinewy and fit, he looked as if he might have just stepped inside to visit a brother, except for his twitchy nervousness and anxious eyes.

'Over 'ere, Miss,' he said in a flat, insistent voice while I was doing one of my long rounds of the room. He kept this up insistently and was so pushy that the other men's cries of 'Miss, can I have a thin brush, Miss?' and 'Can I have a new drawing book, Miss?' were overwhelmed.

As I got delayed, trying to find things and dealing with the register and all the men's demands, I saw him watching me, rubbing his long narrow hands together, then cracking his knuckles and groaning in desperation. He reminded me of a hungry cat.

'I've got to paint this picture,' he said to me, almost breathless with anticipation when I got to him. Just to emphasise how urgent this was, he stood right up against me. He insisted that we turn around, away from the class, so he could tell me quietly, almost in secret. 'I want to paint a picture of a ho,' he said. 'This woman that I know.'

'Righto,' I said, soothingly, but I felt nervous. His intensity and his closeness were alarming.

'Would you like to start by making a drawing?' He looked blank. 'What exactly does this woman look like?

'A bitch.'

'Well, what kind of a bitch?'

He liked that, looked at me for a moment, smiled in something like a spasm revealing two gold incisors, then returned to looking cool again. There was a transparent, plastic tailor's dummy in the art cupboard which no one ever used. I grabbed it as the nearest thing I could see to a human body available for drawing. To my relief, he seemed to like the look of it, particularly relishing the fact that it had no head, arms or legs.

'It's like she's been cut up,' he said, laughing, running his long fingers over it making it squeak. He decided to paint it as the woman he had in mind, complete with a wide black pimp's hat draped on the top.

I set up some sugar paper on a board. He had never drawn anything before so this was slightly ambitious and particularly difficult because of the way reflected light shone on the figure. He immediately decided that he wanted to paint it instead, as if painting were some kind of easy option, slapping over the cracks.

I tried to convince him to draw first and showed him how to measure and look at scale. He got the idea and worked hard for a few minutes but then lost his concentration.

'I don't like doing this,' he said down my ear, threateningly. 'I just come here to make a nice picture to give my woman. I'm seeing her Friday. Gotta have the thing done by Friday.'

I tried to convince him that he should draw and gave

him some clues about using tone. He was mystified, and it wasn't easy to see distinct tones in the dingy light of the prison, with the little light we had refracted through layers of floating dust.

'Friday,' he said angrily. 'I've got to have it this week, finished, a beautiful painting, for her. I want her to see it. I have got to show her.'

'To show her what?' I wondered.

'I want her to learn what will happen to her if she doesn't stop,' he said, making his thin mouth into a hard line. 'If she keeps going with other men for money. She works in private houses in Southall run by Asian men. Mini-cab drivers take them there; the police don't do nothing.'

It seemed odd that he would want to ask the police for help but he was obviously desperate about this woman. He wanted control, and if he couldn't have that, he wanted to hurt her.

He looked at the painting in despair. 'I can't do it, Miss. You do it.'

So I did it, and it was such a relief from walking round the room trying to teach people who didn't want to know that I was happy to be his hired painter for a few days. Besides, he was terribly determined that I would do it.

I compromised by insisting that he make a drawing before I started the painting. I soon heard the usual cry, 'It's all gone wrong, Miss. Look, it's all got messed up!'

He yowled at me, screwed up the drawing and threw it on the floor. I felt like a mother with a screaming toddler, or perhaps Michelangelo with a screaming pope. I showed him how to make a sketch in paint. It was a struggle as the cheap paint faded quickly into the cheap paper, and as they were loose, explorative marks, not worrying too much about the finished result, he was unimpressed and wouldn't try it himself. 'You do it,' was his constant command.

In the end, I did the painting of the dummy 'ho' in the hat almost all by myself, while he watched, fascinated, squeezed up to my shoulder, sniggering occasionally but in an admiring way as if I were doing magic tricks.

His nervousness infected me, and I was afraid that I would now mess the thing up. I wondered what he would do to me if anything did go wrong. Probably just have a howling fit, but he was alarmingly volatile. I was the teacher but he was in control. But I felt there was something sensitive there and I didn't want to block it. Nothing in the textbooks prepared me for testosterone pimps with severe emotional needs.

When she was finished, in all her round, nude glory, he didn't seem to know what to make of it. He almost seemed scared of it.

'It looks a bit rude, Miss,' he said, as if he hadn't noticed that it was naked before. But he was very keen that I should be there at the next lesson. 'Will you be there?' he kept asking. At first no one wanted me. Now I had an acolyte.

I was so distracted by Vere that I fell down on my 'inclusiveness' – or was it 'diversity'? I hardly saw the other men now, but they just kept copying away at their soft-porn images and family photos and didn't complain. I hardly noticed Rupert. The fat, blond middle-aged man sat quietly at the big table in the centre of the room reading tattered old magazines, not bothering anyone.

When I did get to speak to him, it was odd to hear such courteous English, the first privately educated voice I'd heard in there. He seemed to accept everything around him as if it were quite normal for him to be there. He was oddly cheerful and only slightly preoccupied. Being unable to concentrate was common enough, as many of the men in the Scrubs are on remand, awaiting sentence and thinking about court appearances and the problem of explaining themselves to juries, wives and children. Rupert was different because he seemed to be preoccupied with art.

He brought along piles of sketchbooks and folded sheets of paper. They were covered in small sketches and doodles, like something by a child who lies on a carpet and just draws and draws. They showed graffiti-like images, shapes and bottles but also him, lying prone, with a naked woman on top stabbing him with a stiletto heel. In another, he was face down, sprawled out with a woman pushing his face into the ground. There were scenes of whipping, spanking, rampaging snakes, knives and ropes, all done rather roughly in faint pencil, sinking into the thin paper. But there were also some exquisite little drawings, done very expressively, showing a man sitting at a dining table having a family meal with a woman and a young blonde girl. They could have been Dutch genre pictures except there was no joy in them and all the figures were very separate and still.

The young girl appeared again, sometimes lying down with large Roy Lichtenstein-type tears dripping down her face. Then she was attacking him or he was punishing her.

'You made me do it!' the drawings seemed to yell.

'She did make me do it,' he told me quite matter-of-factly, as if the girl had been a fatal trap. He didn't say any more, and I left it alone.

'He's weird. Don't ask him anything,' said John when I asked him if he knew anything about Rupert. 'Nothing must get out about his case,' he said, 'or he might be attacked.'

I remembered the prison dictum which rather casually fits crimes to men: Asians incest, blacks drugs, whites paedophilia. All the middle-aged white men were under suspicion of sex crimes, especially if they were educated and quietly spoken.

Rupert was interested in anatomy so I brought in *Human Anatomy: The Body from the Renaissance to Today,* published by Thames & Hudson. This is a rather macabre tour de force, showing mostly antique exploratory etchings and drawings, often of skeletons posing grotesquely, whilst putting across some kind of a moral message to the viewer. It is both fun and grisly.

He decided he wanted to copy, or get me to copy, the most elaborate drawing in the whole book: a Dutch composition from 1701, stretching over two pages, showing foetal skeletons singing and playing musical instruments. We set up a large sheet of white paper on a board, and he got going with his pencil, totally absorbed.

Although he kept to himself, he managed to get himself elected 'class helper' and came in slightly early to sweep up and empty the bins, for 50p a day. When there was no one about, he liked chatting to me. He told me that he'd been a banker with a large house in Richmond. They had croquet parties in the summer and his wife didn't have to work. He spoke about her with wistful affection, but like an old man whose wife had been dead a long time. They had only been married for two years, and she brought with her a daughter aged fourteen. Rupert had raped this girl continually, but, as he said, 'She wanted it. She was in control.'

The marriage, the house and the croquet lawn were now far beyond his reach.

'My wife won't see me,' he said, as if that was just as it should be. He understood her but felt sorry for her, as if she were mistaken in some way about him. He never expressed regret as if what had happened had been unavoidable. At the same time, he was fascinated by what he'd done, trying to work it out over and over in his drawings.

Having Vere and Rupert together created some

interesting energy, and one morning Vere produced a large pencil drawing he'd done in his cell. It showed him lying on what looked like a prison bed, while above him hovered a heavenly host led by a blonde angel who rather resembled Heather Mills, who was clawing out his heart. It hung from her red talons like a glossy beef tomato, squirting blood over the victim below.

'Has the company psychiatrist seen this?' I said cheekily. He gave me a flash of gold but indicated with a twitch of one eye that he was too keen to get on with painting this scene to bother with jokes.

'You gonna help me paint it,' he said. 'I need a board, where's the paint?'

We stretched a bed sheet over a heavy painting board and found enough paint to start (most of the containers were congealed with old dried paint). We located some passable brushes, borrowed a better quality fine one from Bill's private store, and soon we had a scene of heavenly evisceration in glorious gold and red poster paint, the female angels led by their blonde avenger, swooping down to destroy the hapless male lying prone and captive on the bed. Although I did a lot of it, Vere seemed so fascinated by it that he gained confidence and set to work by himself, 'owning his work', as they said in college, painting a flaming sunset in the sky.

One day, he whispered to me darkly, 'What do you want? I'll get it for you.'

I took a breath. Men on remand can have money sent in, and he was probably quite rich. Some of them have gold bars to match their teeth and huge assets which the Government labours to sequester. What would I like? There was that expensive art course at Heatherley's in Chelsea that I would love to do, and some green silk pyjamas from Selfridges, smooth and heavy as mercury.

'I wouldn't mind some treacle toffees,' I said, knowing he wouldn't let it rest until I had said something, and for some reason the treacle toffees they sold in the Scrubs were very good. It was breaking the rules allowing him to give me anything – probably came under the label 'trafficking' – but I couldn't take sweets seriously.

Prisoners are infantilised, and even confectionery comes into this. Each wing has 'canteen night' one night a week, when they spend their weekly pocket money of £2.50, their basic rate before money for work is added on. Most of them make extra money from work – £1 for cleaning windows and gardening and £1.10 for each of the five education classes they attend – and canteen night is a special event, a chance to spend your pocket money, a bit like going to the tuck shop.

'I'll get you a big bag,' he said.

'Just one or two will do,' I said, but he didn't listen. I could only escape from him by going into the art cupboard, with its black and white Comicon books showing Soviet waterways and factories, or going outside into the corridor on the pretence of seeing old Frank and his murals which never seemed to grow.

Frank was hoping to go to an open prison but he wanted to have a reason for staying in the Scrubs, just in case such a place didn't come up and there was an attempt to shunt him to another hard gaol. The murals would not be finished until he got the word he was going to an open prison, but he never heard anything, so he was stuck to them, like a fly on paper. He said that he genuinely wanted to finish them, and he took pride in them.

'I was a grammar-school boy. I've worked hard all my life and never let anyone down,' he told me, rubbing his large drinker's nose. He said he had been a mining engineer and worked all over the world, until he went into semi-retirement in Venezuela. While he was there he had some trouble getting hold of his pension from the UK. He supported himself by teaching English but because he was so worried about money he had flown back to the UK to sort things out, bringing along a small bag of cocaine at the same time. It was his first offence, but he got six years.

'The funny thing is,' he says brightly, 'while I was on remand I got in touch with the Citizens Advice Bureau and they sorted out my pension difficulties for me right away.'

He had not told his daughters in Manchester about his prison sentence and hoped they would never find out even though this meant losing contact with them for years.

Cut adrift, he was deeply worried about where he would live when he eventually got out. Despite these anxieties he kept up his old courtesy and charm.

'When I get out, can I buy you a cup of tea, can you meet me in town?' he asked. 'Will you do me the honour of coming with me to see the wonderful murals in St Dunstan's Church in Woking? I would love to show them to you.'

To my surprise, I noticed quite a lot of older people around; 10 per cent of foreign-national prisoners in the Scrubs are aged between fifty and seventy. Most of the white people I saw were middle-aged or older, including a former RAF pilot. They are sometimes called the 'Saga Louts' although they are rarely loutish, usually just pensive and sad.

Most are in for carrying drugs. There must be a special group of drug dealers out there trained in the art of persuading elderly law-abiding folk to do recklessly stupid things.

One example of someone acting out of character was Piet, a Boer from Durban, aged fifty-three. With his snub nose and goatee beard he looked like a character painted by Frans Hals. He was a mechanical engineer and a family man until he took to extreme tourism.

'I found that at my age it was very hard to get work,' he said. 'In my line of work, visiting oil rigs and fuel plants, no one wants to employ you after forty-five because they don't want to pay the insurance if there's an accident. In the end I agreed to take the drugs in because I have a five-year-old child to put through school. I thought it would be one trip, easy enough, and I'd use some of the money to have a holiday in London. I never seemed to have enough money or stopped working long enough to have a foreign vacation, and I was hoping to see the Queen.'

He ended up as her full-time guest, seeing nothing of London except the airport.

'At Heathrow, I saw them looking at my luggage and the dog's arse really moving about,' he told me. 'They collapsed my case completely and I saw the packets of drugs roll out, and then I collapsed. I fainted dead away.'

He awoke in HM Customs boarding accommodation at Heathrow and was allowed one phone call to his wife. 'I heard her screaming,' he said. 'She went berserk. "I told you not to do it, you bloody fool," she screamed. "What have you done to us?"'

Like Frank, he keeps his situation secret from his children.

'My youngest daughter thinks I am away on an English course,' he said. 'When I talk to her on the phone, she says, "but Daddy, your English is already very good, you don't need to learn English." I tell her it is an intensive course and I have to do it.'

John made efforts to get more new people into the art room. He went recruiting on the wings and new faces continued to appear. The art room was different now, surprisingly improved by seeing Vere waiting by his bedsheet canvas sighing and moaning until I could give him my undivided attention and Rupert working away silently, scaling up his drawing to giant proportions, laying large sheets of white paper across several tables. I was just relieved that he had not taken a fancy to *The Raft of the Medusa* or the ceiling of the Sistine Chapel.

His work was going to take weeks, and he was completely obsessed with it. He started to copy other pages from the book, including *The Flayed Angel*, by Jacques Gautier d'Agoty, made in 1746, showing a deep dissection of the back muscles under the wings, which look quite strangely normal.

To graffiti, soft porn and comic-book horror, we now added angels – or perhaps winged demons. They came flying out of the minds of angry men who saw themselves as ugly and evil, unworthy of love and respect. I was fascinated how people often with the advantage of good looks, charm and intelligence had ended up in this rump of an art room, and they sometimes asked me the same question. 'What you doin' 'ere, Miss?' they'd say with a mixture of interest and teasing.

Julius didn't have the looks, but he had charm, once you got to know him. He was a regular uninvited visitor to my class – painfully thin, younger than me but looking very old, his black skin wizened and creased by heroin. He had very few teeth and on his head startling upturned corkscrews which reminded me of the Piccaninny in the old Rupert annuals. At first I was scared of him because of his ferocious looks and because he seemed aggressive. He was always asking very pointed questions: 'Why you not married, Miss?', 'Got any kids, didn't no one want you then?'

He investigated my professional disappointments too. 'Why didn't you make it big, Miss?' he once asked. 'Why weren't you one of the ones to make it? Why aren't you appearing on afternoon TV?' He'd picked up this style of questioning in Fatima's 'Skills for Life' lessons.

In a recent class they had asked a teacher if he was a 'batty boy' and forced him out of the room in tears. It seemed more like 'Skills for Getting Yourself Killed' to me.

The best way to deal with this kind of confrontation was humour, the great currency of prison. One day, Julius was looking at a theatre programme I'd brought in from the new production of *The Lord of the Rings*. I said, 'Did I see you on stage last night?'

He grinned slowly, showing his few splayed teeth, then fell about laughing.

Vere began to talk to me about his vicious angels, the origin of his vividly painted blonde demons. He told me about his childhood, blighted by a particularly unpleasant form of racism which was new to me. Born in London of Caribbean parents, his father was an electrician, his mother a machinist. They were comfortably off, and he might have done well, but his parents rejected him.

'There was a lot of tension at home, but I got a particularly hard time because I am very black,' he told me. 'As I grew up, I got racial abuse from both my parents. When my father was angry, he said I wasn't his son as I was too dark. There is a caste system based on skin colour in West Indian culture, they think like that: that the blacker you are, the closer you are to the Devil. My mother disliked my appearance. She said I was "black like Satan." I always felt bad about myself.'

Coupled with this, he also experienced the traditional Caribbean way of child rearing.

'There was no history of crime in my family,' he said, 'but my Dad was very violent to us. He'd drag me out of bed in the middle of the night and lay in to me with his belt. I was terrified of him because you could never tell when one of his violent moods would flare up. My mother also imposed strict discipline on me and my sister. She would whip us with a cane. We were scared of her too.'

He took to comfort eating and got very fat but did well in school, always in the B group, and he was popular. As he plied me with toffees, I saw him as the amiable fat boy, generous to everyone in the playground.

He got back at his parents by stealing. 'My sister and I both started shoplifting at a very young age,' he said.

At fifteen, he was sent to Borstal. That was the end of his schooling, although he got a CSE in biology while he was in there which helped him to maintain a small shred of confidence.

After Borstal, his life was worse. 'I really wanted to go to prison so that I could escape from home,' he said.

From his late teens he had seen prison as a refuge. Inside prison, he prospered and learned all about crime. Instead of biology books and art classes, he learned about drugs, burglary, theft, fraud and pimping.

'Crime was quite natural to me,' he said rather shyly, half embarrassed. 'I just wanted to get rich, and crime was the only way I could do it. I was more easily accepted on the crime scene than anywhere else.'

I asked many Afro-Caribbean and mixed-race men how they got into crime. They all saw their lack of literacy as a factor, but they blamed the literacy problem on unhappiness in childhood. 'If I had had a different home and different parents I could have done well,' Vere said bitterly.

Sometimes I met Muslim youths who were also highly

discontented with their elders. One lively Pakistani, inside for drugs, had recently discovered an Asian alternative comedian who attacked the attitudes of his parents' generation, particularly how they dealt with their children.

'They are always beating their kids,' he told me. 'This guy said a young boy told his father that if he hit him again he would call the police. Call them, said the father, it will take them ten minutes to get here and I can do a lot of damage in ten minutes.'

He told this story laughing but his eyes glittered with resentment. But men often said that kind of thing reluctantly, as if it was extremely painful to blame their parents.

'It's easier for me to think that I had a good background. I prefer to blame myself,' Isaac said. 'I don't like the bitter feelings I often have against my parents, but when I think about the life I might have had, going to college, it is too painful for me to deal with and sometimes I hate my father.'

Like Vere, he also came from what he called a 'hard-working background'. His father was in construction while his mother worked in accounts, and they owned their own home in South London.

'I could read by the time I went to school,' he said. 'My parents were never worried about me until I got to thirteen when I dropped out of school completely and began to get involved with drugs.'

At that time, the family moved from London back to his father's home in Tobago. Isaac was sent to a private school run by Seventh Day Adventists. That was the start of his real troubles.

'It was strict, and I was way behind academically after my English school where they had been much more free and easy,' he said. 'I couldn't keep up with the others, and

I became very upset about going to school. Eventually I refused to go, and my father got tired of beating me and told me to stay at home and look after the animals, which is what I did. He lost interest in me after that. I turned into a kind of farm boy, just happy that the pressure was off.'

When the family returned to the UK three years later, there was no chance of him joining mainstream education. 'When I came back to England, I had no education and no chance of any job except labouring,' he said. 'I got jobs on building sites; I was a hod carrier, but I found it hard to get work. As I don't look enough like a white man I didn't fit in easily anywhere and when they built Wembley stadium they employed all foreign workers at rock-bottom wages and we got laid off anyway. I drifted into the drug culture, and it was much easier to fit in with the drugs scene. When I got on the smack I needed quick money, and I had no way to get it other than by crime. Since then I have had a life of petty crime.'

Many of the men said that selling drugs was their only way of making fast money to get the right shoes, flash clothes and more drugs. This was the lifestyle, a parody of success that they craved. But they also said that they only felt emotionally secure within a surrogate family of fellow 'druggies'.

For many, prison continued as an extended version of this surrogate family, and life on the inside was pretty similar to the one they'd left behind on the streets. After all, supplies are irregular on the outside *and* the inside, and it takes ingenuity in both places to get them and survive. In prison, with a bit of patience, you can get most of the things you need. People cooperate, and there is much less violence than out on the street.

Bill was the same. A long-term drug dealer, he had never known any other kind of life. Prison was his home, and he often appeared to be a genial host, providing happily for his guests. The other men bitched about him, complaining about his smelly dreadlocks, because he was seen as too wily and selfish, too skilled at getting what he wanted, but he was an integral part of the Scrubs culture.

When my ear problem returned, Bill quickly appeared with a brand-new bottle of 'Waxsol' ear drops for me. Deals had been done on the wing. Sadly, the drops were a waste of effort – no use for an infection. Bill couldn't save me from the rigours of the outside world, such as dealing with the NHS. I had to take a Monday morning off to go through the rigmarole of trying to make an appointment with the doctor. When I finally spoke to a human being, she told me I would have to wait until Friday before I could have an appointment.

Five days is a long time when you are in pain, but by Friday the infection had almost gone. I went along to the surgery anyway because getting an appointment was such an achievement. When I arrived, the receptionist told me they had no record of any appointment; in fact, it couldn't have been made as they only book patients three days in advance at the most. My evidence was that they had said a locum would see me, and a locum was in that afternoon. Still, I felt like a lying impostor as I sat and waited until the end of surgery time when the doctor 'might' see me.

I sat among the old magazines, plastic toys and decrepit old men, listening to an oleaginous voice from an overhead television asking if we were suffering from debt-induced stress and offering to help for a large fee. There was also the less soothing voice of the receptionist snapping at veiled Muslim women. I watched them scurry away like frightened mice.

The doctor was Chinese, affable, but told me rather impatiently that as the infection was diminishing there was little he could do. We were both sorry that nothing could be done, and I went home. Sometimes prison seemed a decidedly more rational place than the teeming toe-treading town outside.

After a month in the art room I got a chance to do other things. Fran asked me to help with the prison magazine, and I began teaching an NUJ course, with journalism embedded in literacy. Fran hated the press, as she saw it as 'an agent of capitalism, spouting lies', but she seemed glad that I had been a 'real' journalist, able to bring that experience to teaching.

She invited me to have lunch in the hospital canteen with her and Gerald, who was a senior tutor and the department's union official. He had retired after a life of teaching in private schools and was now doing four days a week in the Scrubs. Pugnacious in spite of his cerise muffler, to hear him rant took me back to my student days.

'I'm a Communist,' said Fran intensely, over my half-heated cod Mornay in glutinous sauce. She only ever ate salad and rice. 'I've always seen myself as a Che Guevara type of person. I would always side with the prisoners. I tell them get on with it, just don't get caught. They are where they are because they have been robbed by the upper classes of this country. Do you realise that most of Britain is still in the hands of just a few former slave-owners?'

She didn't really require an answer, only a nod and a murmur of approval. Her speech patterns, with their rising cadence at the end of each line and the frequent soft, murmured 'yeah?' reminded me of speech I'd heard in women's groups in the early 1980s.

I could see that Fran wanted to make real changes for the men in prison and, like me, she was still struggling to make something of her own life at the same time.

'I have got so many things I want to achieve,' she told me, picking at a veggie burger. 'I've got to make something of myself now before it is too late.'

Gerald, whose mother had been a Tory magistrate, had grown up Old Labour and was sad about the way things had gone, but he blamed the workers: 'Most of the *Sun*-reading class support the BNP,' he said bitterly. 'I would be happier if they didn't have the vote.'

Listening to them, I realised that it is probably hard to be in teaching if you are not left-wing. I didn't want to get into any hot political debate because they seemed to like me and wanted to befriend me, and I was extremely grateful. At the time friends seemed to be about as rare as spotting a white middle-class man on a bus – or in a prison.

I would have liked to have had lunch with Comfort, but she was on a perpetual diet, although she didn't get any slimmer so she must have been eating at home, where she shared a flat with her mother. But I had a few friends at last, and even Fatima became more amenable. After observing me coldly from a distance for a few weeks like a territorial cat, she started talking to me as if we were good friends. One day, she threw her long boney arms around me for 'big hugs' and asked me to attend a training day on 'Speaking and Listening Skills'.

This was held at one of the dingier hotels in Bloomsbury. Despite the £50 fee, the day began with a cup of coldish coffee and a fruit Shrewsbury biscuit. Not a chocolate croissant in sight, a bad sign.

We gathered in a very large, hot room with vertical drapes: ten people, nine of them middle-aged women, adorned with name badges – first names only of course. Eric, the only man present, who worked for the YMCA in Great Yarmouth, was large and elderly with a lot of hair sprouting from the top of his nose. Sheila and Grace, two well-dressed middle-class women, had devised the whole day and had composed the large shiny folder that went with it, which was almost too big to carry. Former teachers, they looked happy and affluent, people who had found a good way out of teaching into the education conference business and had never looked back.

We all had to introduce ourselves with a team-building 'icebreaker'. We formed a circle, said who we were – first names only again, lest any adult formality should creep in. The person next in line had to remember your name and the name of the person before, and before that and so on, like the old game of My Grandmother's Fan.

It was the sort of thing I would have hated when I was six, and I saw some people looking anxious and uncomfortable. But obviously if you enter the public sector you have to get used to playing party games in public – in fact, they become a normal part of your professional life.

Once transformed into 'buddies', we were allowed back to our places. Sheila and Grace set up a large flip chart and introduced the day's theme: 'Speaking and Listening'. To describe this process, they employed words from therapy and American Evangelism; it was going to be a day of 'sharing', 'affirming', 'setting boundaries', 'mirroring' and 'awareness-raising'.

Grace also suggested that we should 'brainstorm' some ideas. At that, a fat young woman from Ipswich who said she was in 'military education', got really upset.

'I really think that we as teachers should be very aware and concerned about this sort of thing,' she said, her voice cracking with emotion. Sheila and Grace gave her a very glossy smile and attempted to press on.

'I'm not staying here,' said the girl, pronouncing 'stay'

like 'sty'. 'I've not got no time for that kind of discriminatory language. It should have been stopped years ago.'

The ladies in charge cooed sympathetically, totally unruffled, like very experienced primary-school teachers, which perhaps they were. The rest of us kept quiet. Getting no real support, the girl subsided and we got down to some 'pair-work'. One person had to talk while another listened, observed by the others who then made critical feedback on their oral and auditory skills.

At my table they decided that I was a poor listener because I didn't use enough body language or 'mirroring' while the other person was speaking. I toyed with the idea of walking out. I could spend the day in a gallery, no one would know. But like the girl from Ipswich, I sat on, like a good child.

Next we had to plan out an imaginary lesson using a storyboard, illustrations and short pieces of information. I thought I'd do a biography of Van Gogh using slide illustrations for each stage of his life. Grace seemed really surprised and delighted with my idea. I realised why when Eric said he was going to do his presentation on 'assessment'. Did people really do storyboards about that and how would he illustrate it? I felt shocked.

The lunch was meagre: no wine, squashed sandwiches, a few cold chicken legs and piles of kiwi fruit. On my way to the loo I saw another group lining up for a hot lunch, glasses of wine in hand, men and women together, having a high old time. Perhaps they were bankers, advertising consultants, travel reps, even journalists. Obviously not teachers. I felt as cross as a cat whose owner has just turned vegetarian.

Back in the big room, I was surprised that no one moved about doing any networking but sat quietly at their own tables. I tentatively changed tables to try to talk to other people, but the woman I lighted on stared at me as if I was potty. As no one else had moved it seemed like a positive insult to the table I'd left behind. When I returned to my seat, there was very little speaking or listening going on. No one said anything until Eric saw me take out a copy of *Private Eye*. 'Do people really read that?' he said, sounding shocked.

At 4 p.m., as it drew to a close, I asked Grace for an extra copy of the giant shiny folder, which caused some jealous grumbling.

I gave one to Fatima and got more big hugs. The other became a second coffee table and remains unopened.

5

The Education Department was short-staffed, with teachers and managers constantly off sick. The college had budgeted for 6 per cent absenteeism, but the real figure was nearer 20 per cent, so I had to cover other classes, usually literacy, raising my basic twenty hours to about thirty-five a week.

In these extra classes I got to better know 'White Van Man' and his black contemporaries. In prison, *Vir vehiculus albus* is surprisingly rare and often hard to see as he is almost the same colour as the walls, a kind of seasick green – sometimes with added shades of blue and jaundiced yellow.

'Stabbin', Miss,' he'd usually say carelessly when I asked why he was there. Or 'Well all I done was like kick this pub door in' – the implication being that he had somehow been misunderstood.

Unlike the black British men I talked to, these white oiks had not come from childhoods steeped in violence, and they did not have strong identity problems, but they had suffered from poverty both financial and cultural. Their main problem in class was an inability to concentrate. They fell asleep a lot as they usually sat up all night watching television, and they were almost palpably scared of their own language. 'You are speaking Old English, Miss,' they'd say quite seriously. Or, 'That's posh talk that is.'

One afternoon we were reading something which contained some new words: 'grimace', 'gravely', 'supposed', 'conclude', 'expire', and 'determine'. While the Africans and Poles wrote them down studiously the white lads made it clear they thought they were outrageously eccentric: 'Grimace? Never 'eard of it, Miss.' 'I'll never say that, Miss! Grimace? When am I going to say that?'

Acquiring a wide vocabulary was just not part of their culture; words were for the 'other', the middle classes, people from a different world, as much value to them and as little taught as ballet.

Sam Wilkins, forty-five, lard-white, heavily tattooed over acres of flesh, was one of the stars of Fran's Advanced English class. He had acquired seven exam passes along with ten years for homicide. Apart from his exam passes, he had taken part in Fran's sound-editing course and hoped to take a history degree with the Open University when he moved on to Parkhurst or a place with other lifers. A former pupil of Holland Park Comprehensive, where Tony Benn sent his children in the 1960s, he didn't quite have the Benn home background, and while they went into the Cabinet and journalism, he went to prison for armed robbery.

He'd first done time aged eighteen. Since then, he'd had a life inside, just as his parents had probably envisaged for him.

'I think about 90 per cent of my friends' fathers were gaol birds,' he said. 'My old man was a well-known gangster and racketeer; my godfather was Michael McEvoy who got twenty-five years for his part in the Brinks Mat robbery at Heathrow in 1983. Another close family friend was part of the Kray Gang. I had that special crime pedigree – we were up there at the top, the elite, and education wasn't uppermost on our list of priorities. The idea was to get rich through crime like all the people you and your parents most admired. The alternative to that was boring, menial, degrading jobs. I just didn't come from a culture that took schooling seriously. We never saw education as a way out.'

He could not remember anyone in school or any other area of his life ever trying to change this attitude. 'Middle-class people admired us,' he said. 'They thought the Krays were romantic and they loved *EastEnders*. They wanted to be like us. Until I committed a murder, I had no idea that there was any other way to live, a different kind of life. Until I came to prison and met you people in Education I didn't know that you could make learning the foundation of your life. I had no sense of something of value that wasn't money – of doing something for me that would be mine, that no one could take away.'

He wanted a go at the same education that the rich middle classes give their children. But leaving prison, changing his life outside, would be another matter.

As I got to know the prisoners, I began to realise that it was absurd to expect them to be able to change easily. Those 'mind-forged manacles' had been there often from the very start of their lives. Prisoners struggled with the idea of change and often wrote down their ideas. One typical poem contained the lines:

Can I change or do I have to stay
The same? Can I go somewhere else
Or do I have stay?

They'd almost always write about leaving prison with something like existential dread:

> My *heart is kicking, time is ticking*
> *And soon the bell will ring.*
> *The gates will open.*
> *I'll step out there and know*
> *If life can mean a thing.*

A surprising number of them liked writing poetry, something they would probably never do on the outside. I contacted a well-known poet – at least I spoke to 'his people' – about getting him to come in to the prison. I knew he spent a lot of time touring the UK giving poetry readings. Witty and amusing, obviously a good performer, he would have inspired the men with their writing. His people said that he had already 'done prison'. So he wasn't doing it again. This gave me my 'Alcatraz' feeling, as if we were all on an island, cut off from the mainstream of education for good. Perhaps at best the men were only ever novelty value.

Jim Garvey, aged twenty-eight, was on his eighth prison stretch since the age of eighteen. In for 'stabbin', he was born long after that Kray-worshipping culture had faded from fashion. Handsome, although pallid and listless, good at writing short pieces about himself, it always seemed odd to me that he was mouldering inside. 'It was poverty in my childhood,' he said, sounding disgusted and hopeless.

His father, a violent alcoholic, had left when Jim was five, leaving the family with no financial support. 'When my younger sister was little, my mother had part-time jobs and I had to act as carer,' he said. 'Sometimes I had to cook a meal for us all with only £2.50 on the table. I managed it, but we mainly lived on corned beef. It was poverty that made me different to the other boys, and it wrecked my chances.'

Like Isaac, a change of school in his early teens had been the crisis point. His primary school had been fine but then his mother sent him to a Catholic secondary school in Richmond where there were a lot of middle-class boys and he couldn't fit in.

'I hated the uniform; my accent was all wrong,' he said. 'I was quite small until I was about seventeen and I got bullied.'

He dropped out at thirteen, got involved in petty crime and became dependent on drugs. When he was first sent to a young-offenders centre two years later, he passed three GCSEs at Grade C. He was proud to say that these were taken as straight exams with no coursework. In prison, he has gained seventeen exam certificates plus NVQs in fitness training.

Like Sam, Jim saw that he must change his life, but he only came to that conclusion after he'd been to prison. Educationalists on the outside had never offered him any incentive to learn. I suspected that he'd been afraid of school, and at the same time, like most of the English prisoners, he'd been a victim of that strange lack of confidence among teachers and the blanking of our culture which is now part of our national psyche.

He'd probably been taught by the kind of teacher I heard in the prison library one day telling someone, 'I am doing a degree in English at the moment. I am reading *Rebecca* by Daphne du Maurier. It's really good. I'm also reading some classics as well now. I know that sounds like really crap, but some of them are quite nice.'

White Van Man was generally very easy to teach, if he could keep awake, and compared with the tensions of the art room my English lessons seemed remarkably relaxed. Between six and eight men would meekly troop in to the small airless room with its tiny barred window, sit quietly around a table and remain attentive while I took the lesson, writing on a large whiteboard behind me.

Prison is a low-tech place for low-tech people – no electronic whiteboards or even flip charts, strictly a paper-and-pens place. It reminded me of my own schooldays, and I often reached back to the 1970s for my A-level material. I was well served by the notes I had made then, given out by Mr Higgs our English teacher. He been reviled by the stodgy Midlands boys in the class, for his rumpled suits and mildly anti-war attitudes. He had been somewhat anti-First World War, in line with the poets he was teaching.

I tried the men in the lower-level group on Wilfred Owen and Siegfried Sassoon, but they were non-committal, not really interested. Gas attacks on the Western Front long ago must have seemed as nothing compared to going to court next week and facing ten years inside.

When I tried to introduce them to a bit of Kipling, Andy, a scraggy-haired, whey-faced white lad, kept whining as if he had a shrapnel wound:

'It's too hard, Miss. It's too hard. Can't we watch a film?'

Like training a bunch of raw recruits, it was hard going at first. Although he must have been the descendant of generations of cannon fodder, Andy didn't even respond to Gunga Din. The North-West passage meant nothing to him. He put his head on his spindly arms and seemed to be about to die but revived a bit when I put on a recording of Simon Russell Beale reading 'If', Kipling's great blockbuster.

They responded to 'If' as if it was a lump of tobacco, sitting silent, misty-eyed, entranced and calm; as if it were addressed to them individually, appealing to their sentimental sense of themselves as men capable of risk, honour and noble things as yet undone. They all wanted copies of it to keep in their cells.

They were in such a swoon about it that I got them to try C. P. Cavafy's great poem, 'Sailing to Ithaca', which is more subtle than the Kipling, with life presented as a slow exotic journey rather than a *Boy's Own* adventure.

They didn't say much, so at first I thought they hadn't grasped it. It turned out they had understood it and were so satisfied by it that they didn't need to talk about it. It was like the sort of shared contentment you get after a good Sunday lunch, or perhaps, as they would say, 'a shag'. We got Groot to make more photocopies to take back to the cells.

It was often difficult to get them to speak. The only people who could express themselves confidently were the occasional middle-aged, middle-class white men, including an elderly ex-pat who edited an English-language newspaper in the Philippines, inside for passport fraud, and the Africans who relished language, uninhibited by class issues.

No matter how poor or pestilential their background, the Africans had all somehow got a good basic education; they could express themselves fluently and could concentrate. They were also avid for newspapers and political debate.

'They are not creative enough,' said Fran, who disapproved of them because they had learned things by rote and liked taking notes.

The Africans also had what many white teachers strangely see as an exaggerated respect for the teacher. They would sit up straight paying attention as if I had an electric cattle prod in my plastic bag. International drug dealers and fraudsters from Nigeria, often large men, would look really scared and sometimes mortified if I asked them a direct question. They dreaded not being able to answer correctly.

As someone inexperienced at classroom management, I wasn't complaining about that, and I never heard anyone criticise the white working-class men for being ignorant or unable to write simple sentences. That was one of the many conundrums of British education – learning itself was seen as wrong and disruption as creative. The Africans still belonged to the culture of my parents and grandparents, when there was such a thing as formal education, conducted by formal people. The white lads were the product of modern education methods, and their failure ignored or attributed entirely to social factors.

Comfort agreed with me, but these ideological issues were not worth bringing up at work as they were so divisive.

She passed me two of her morning classes to give her more time for the endless form-filling and forward-planning that teaching seemed to involve. All the teachers needed extra time for administration, which stopped me feeling that I really wanted to take on the full role.

To teach Comfort's lower intermediate groups I had to concentrate more on the nuts and bolts of language. The idea of grammar was nearly as frightening a prospect as maths. I had never done any in school, and it was as arcane to me as chemistry. I took some enjoyment from using *A Basic Course in English* by Walter D. Wright, published in 1961, and a book by Ronald Ridout, which was even earlier and contained such gems as 'The policeman went for a tramp in the woods' and 'Writers of Tolstoy's calliper are hard to find.' The modern books were bland and quirk-free, with no sign of individual authorship, but I would amuse myself with unintentionally interesting bits, such as the line in a simple punctuation exercise: 'My father who used to be a successful businessman is trying to be a bus driver.' I know the feeling, I thought, and what a story lies behind that simple sentence!

I tried to take it slowly, not to be gentle with the pupils but so as not to scare myself, but it is alarming to teach always just one page ahead. You never know if some bright spark is going to ask you a question about the page after that one.

This can work the other way too; the Africans had studied English grammar as small boys, and the East Europeans learned it as teenagers. Many prisoners in the Scrubs speak at least two languages, so if you get a good group you can get them to help you.

'Oh, that's what it means by "the predicate,"' you say lightly, as they explain it to you. 'Now let's have a look at transformational grammar. What is all this about the verb taking, or not taking an object? Hands up who can tell me what that means?'

If a show of teacherly superiority is needed, you can always fox them with jokes of the 'Eats Shoots and Leaves' variety, which they can never understand without a lot of drawings on the board. The same goes for other punning jokes: A bear goes into a bar and says 'Could I have a pint of [long silence] lager please?' 'Fine,' says the bartender, 'but why the big pause?' They never get those, and you will always be at an advantage.

As many of them had studied languages before I was worried about boring them. I would often see Mr Petrov, secretly and compulsively doing Sudoku under his exercise book. An Estonian geologist, who had worked for a large investment company in Africa, he was inside for smuggling drugs in from Kenya, although he insisted he had been set up and had not known about the extremely valuable contents of his briefcase.

I saw others take refuge in daydreaming. When Abdulla, a forklift truck driver from Afghanistan, got bored, he wrote poetry in Urdu, the beautiful curlicues stretching across his pad of cheap graph paper.

'This is from the work of a scholar who lived in London in 1938 and dreamed of a separate Muslim state next to India,' he told me quietly. 'He returned to see the new Pakistan but died shortly after.'

I could see that he constantly travelled through this foreign landscape in his head, inured for a while against the ugliness of the Scrubs.

He was gentle and passive but sat next to drug smugglers from Somalia and Nigeria who were wildly indignant at being locked up by the Queen of England when they were only plying their usual trade in her fair land.

'In Holland, drugs are free,' said the Nigerian, puzzled to get eight years for bringing in four kilos of cocaine. 'In Amsterdam, the judge will wag his finger at you and tell you "Don't do it again."'

'You could destroy a lot of people with that,' said Abdulla, raising his dreamy eyes.

'Destroy? No, it's to enjoy,' said the Nigerian, and everyone laughed.

The Nigerian looked terrified when I asked him straight questions, as teacher, but sometimes I sat back and let him turn into an entertainer, describing his life in the prison, naming the different wings for their different characteristics: B for beatings, C for Kalashnikovs (sic), D for drugs, and E, hopefully, for Exit. This, with his exuberant delivery, big, booming African voice, which Comfort particularly disliked, caused hilarity. If I let him, he came to life, extolling his life's work:

'In Peshawar, between Afghanistan and Pakistan, you can take through 20 kilos of cocaine and get away with it,' he said instructively. 'If you get caught, the UN now provide free food for prisoners in Pakistan. You can get meat every day.'

He had been in prison all over the world, but, despite this he came to the UK to 'do business' and was granted a two-year visa.

'They didn't check my past,' he said but added that he would never be able to return to legitimate business when he got out. 'Once you are in prison you are like a woman who has twin babies,' he bellowed profoundly. 'Afterwards, she wants to fuck with her man again, she try to look pretty, put on her make-up, but he says what are you going to do about your big belly that I can see sticking right out there? Try as she might, she cannot change her shape back to what it was.'

But he was not really worried about his new shape. 'My life is very good now,' he said. 'I am quite happy here.'

Not all Africans were so content with their situation. The crime wave that is Nigeria swept up unlikely people. Mr Bando, aged about seventy, was keen on reading novels in English, usually by Chinua Achebe. He should probably have been in a higher group but was too depressed for much participation.

One day he asked me for a dictionary. I said he'd have to go to the library as teachers weren't allowed to bring stuff in for inmates.

'I want one for myself,' he said, his voice cracking.

I asked him if any of his friends or relations could bring him one, but he hadn't had a single visitor during his two years inside.

He'd once run a small electrical business in Abuja, before he'd got involved with some kind of passport fraud. Now he was thousands of miles away from home, his family were left struggling, and none of them could afford to visit.

I asked the Chaplaincy if they could organise a visitor for him. But prison visiting is not a fashionable job these days, not many people have the time or commitment to do it. Eventually they got him a visit but he turned it down.

'I just want to see someone from my own family,' he told me wretchedly. But after that he would smile fondly at me and call me 'My Miss Jane', as if I were a surrogate grand-daughter.

Some of my classes with these groups started out innocently, but very often the reality of the situation would intrude and I would be left feeling rattled and annoyed. On a rare warm day in June, the small classroom with its barred window already suffocating, I set a lesson about writing holiday postcards. The Africans couldn't quite get the idea as it meant curtailing their loquaciousness.

Their cards went along the lines of 'My compliments of the Season, best wishes to you my friend – how are you? I hope your life is going smoothly, if so, praise be to God Almighty. Yours truly.'

A discussion about holidays seemed appropriate as a lot of them had arrived as tourists to London, or rather as consumers visiting the cocaine capital of Europe. In the short time between leaving Heathrow and being arrested, only a few had ever ventured beyond the capital.

One man told me he had come to London for a holiday with his wife and children, but he had never heard of Trafalgar Square or Buckingham Palace. He'd made straight for Oxford Street where he said drugs were easily on sale.

I was often astonished at the lack of self-awareness of these globe-trotting criminals. Rubin, from St Vincent, in the Grenadines, inside for street robbery in West London, had once been on holiday in Scandinavia with his mother.

'Sweden and Norway are controlled countries,' he said wistfully. 'There are not many foreigners, people are friendly, and there is hardly any crime. You can just walk down the street without worrying. I'd like to live there all the time.'

If I had been drinking a cup of tea when he said this I might well have spluttered it all over him.

The theme of the class was holidays, but the only thing I recognised as a traditional holiday came from an elderly Jamaican with a stick, who talked about Dunn's River Falls in his homeland. He gave such a rich, fond description of the place and rafting through some caves that we were suddenly almost tearful with longing as if we'd often been there ourselves.

As we were mainly talking about holidays in the UK, I wondered if they could name any famous contemporary Brits. Piet, the unfortunate tourist from Durban, suggested Queen Victoria. I suggested he was a bit out of date.

'Well, Queen Victoria must have had some family,' said Rubin, helpfully, but he couldn't come up with any. When we finally got to the present queen, he launched into a tirade against the monarchy.

'She takes all our taxes,' he said, 'all the money in the country goes to her.' The others agreed.

We got to Gordon Brown. 'He must earn millions. He is the big man,' said Rubin, banging his fist on the table.

I would often hear these primitive views of politics, often laced with complex conspiracy theories, a mixture of deep culture and information from CNN, Al Jazeera and jihadi websites, now carried across the world in the luggage of these new global travellers.

I became aware that there are many myths about Britain alive in the developing world, for instance that everything is free here and degrees are very easy to get. I felt mortified when one young prisoner who had been a student at London University told me, 'loads of people come here because they know it is much easier to get through school here and easier to get a university degree here than anywhere else in Europe. Your educational standards are much lower than Germany.'

He spoke politely, like a child, just telling me the truth, without realising how it might make me feel.

I often felt strangely riled by their complete lack of knowledge about the place they had struggled so hard to reach. Boris Johnson has described London as 'a world in a city'. True enough, and many of the prisoners think that London is Britain, with nothing beyond it. Some even think that they have 'London' passports.

Many wanted to be in Britain, or London, but they despised it. Time and again foreign prisoners would say to me, almost reproachfully, 'you have no culture. There is no culture here.'

Britain is reputed by many to be an extinct culture, a vacancy, a verdant space for them to occupy.

After a few months I was given one of Gerald's Friday classes, as he only wanted a four-day week. This was my first experience of facing a really able group. I quickly realised that in prison I would probably teach a broader range of students to a higher level than would be possible in school, because the discipline is so tight, with the Governor in the old role of headmaster with the big stick, and with no one talking about 'targets'. There are advantages to being in a kind of Alcatraz, largely forgotten and ignored.

Free of a burdensome curriculum I could toss things into the air to see how they landed. We covered the execution of Saddam Hussein ('Saddam, From Monster to Martyr'), Fukuyama's idea about the End of History which had proved premature, tackled global warming, AIDS, the atomic bomb, North Korea, Madonna adopting African babies and the war in Iraq. You could never tell what would spark them off or why. I had to find out by experience. Things I thought would interest them, such as World AIDS Day and even a moving piece of prose such as 'When Did You Last See Your Father?' by Blake Morrison seemed to leave them bored, uninterested. Fathers were a contentious issue to most of the men, but none of them seemed to relate to the father in that one – the culture of middle-class England in the late 1950s was obviously as remote to them as the Pharaohs.

A vivid eyewitness account of the immediate aftermath of the Aberfan disaster, by Laurie Lee, meant nothing to them either. I gave that to them not realising that something I remember painfully from my childhood had turned into just another page of history, and many of them had witnessed terrible suffering in their own lives or came from places where children's lives were cheap.

Yet their response to something more abstract – the role of the critic in modern society – was ridiculously highly charged with a lot of shouting.

I showed them Stanley Kubrick's film *A Clockwork Orange,* the only film ever to be banned by its own director, which predicted a future breakdown of civil society and the rise of consumerism and alienation. I had completely forgotten just how violent it was, and during the graphic rape scenes I felt very uncomfortable, wedged into a small airless room with a lot of male criminals. So did they: the Africans walked out in disgust, calling the film 'obscene', while a black Briton said that ideas like that shouldn't be in a film, they should be in the theatre. 'This is not what films are for,' he said furiously. 'They are supposed to be entertainment.'

Mr Alphons was a large, bespectacled mixed-race man who'd spent most of his forty years locked up – first in a children's home and then prison. He walked with a stick since he'd had his feet scalded in a turf war over crack cocaine. He shouted a lot in discussion and often hobbled out of the room in a rage, slamming the door behind him. Now he was mad with me for saying that in the film the burning of books by one violent character was a deliberately emotive image.

'No, it isn't,' he yelled, 'the guy just wanted to wreck the room, it meant nothing at all – why are we even talking about this, it's just a film. I don't want to sit here talking about fucking films.'

He left, struggling past legs and feet with his stick, slamming the door, rattling the glass in the corridor window.

'Leave us the glass in the door next time,' said Danny when Mr Alphons came back in. A muscular youth with pumped-up biceps, Danny was serving twelve years for armed robbery. His brother was also inside for the same crime. Between them they were said to be worth millions. He told me he was also known as Manouch, but in the criminal underworld chiefly as 'M'.

'As in *Dial M for Murder*?' I said. He looked at me a little askance. Well, aged about twenty-three, he could hardly be expected to be a fan of 1950s murder mysteries set in Maida Vale.

His remark about the glass led to more cursing. Mr Alphons, who was always addressed formally, perhaps because he was older or because he was so touchy, seemed to detest Danny, but everyone else saw them as something of a double act.

'If it's just an effing film, why are you so excited?' said Danny calmly, when we'd all settled down again. 'What would you do if we were talking about something serious, man?' At this, Mr Alphons became enraged and struggled out, slamming the door again. When he returned, I wondered if by creating a film like that Kubrick had helped to bring about the kind of society of which he claimed to be afraid. This question caused a mass exit to the loo with a lot of shouting. But later Danny wrote a piece about the film in *Free Time,* commenting on the 'cold ruthlessness' of the street gangs depicted in the film and saying that it 'didn't seem to be too far from the violence culture that we seem to have fallen into.'

This group would try anything. They included Peter, a courteous black youth who had been getting on well in the building society where he worked until he had gone in for fraud, and Hardip, a Sikh in a blue headscarf rather than a turban, with a cut-glass English accent, who'd been caught posing as a doctor.

I got them to read Sheridan's *The Rivals.* We had a session on Malapropisms, a bit like a traditional grammar-school class, and they took up the word immediately with great relish. Danny, with his tattooed wrestler's arms bulging from under his short-sleeved vest, played Lydia Languish. Mr Alphons played Lucy the maid, perhaps giving her a less carefree slant than usual, while Peter played Mrs Malaprop.

As he spoke her famous mangled words, worthy of any FE college administrator, one of Peter's friends came in and stood behind his chair, patiently adding extra complicated knots to his dreadlocks. An Irishman who'd recently appeared in Education came into the room to join us without any permission, squeezing himself in and trying to distract us with his strange rapid banter. He was given the part of Sir Lucius O'Trigger and was so baffled and alarmed that he quickly disappeared from the room and never came back.

Just before I'd arrived in the prison, Only Connect, an arts company which helps 'people at risk of criminality', had produced *Of Mice and Men*, from the novel by John Steinbeck. It had been performed in the prison chapel with Danny and Peter in the leading roles. To get it on had been a constant struggle with Security. Two men had been removed from the cast at short notice, and an order had gone out from the Governor that all the men would be locked down by 7.30 p.m. sharp, 'even if they were performing'.

'Terrible people who've done filthy things' were not really supposed to be up there performing – that fissure between Education and the prison staff constantly tearing open. But despite that the play had been deemed a great success. For the men taking part, who had never been in a play before, or gone near a theatre, it had been perhaps the most rewarding thing they'd done educationally for years.

'Before I was in that play, I never thought I would ever remember words of more than two syllables,' Danny told me. 'All the time I was rehearsing, I kept thinking, "I can't be doing this, this isn't me, I can't act!" But by that time it was too late.'

In his role of a cowboy he had sported the tightest pair of jeans ever seen in the chapel or probably anywhere in the prison. He had also helped to find other inmates willing to have a go and get on stage.

'Intrepid volunteers', he called them. 'Taking part meant I had done something I thought was impossible for me,' he said. 'It proved the old saying that if you put your mind to it, you can accomplish anything.'

Drama seemed to provide a unique release for them and a rapid way of gaining self-esteem from learning. I could see how they relished the Restoration play, laughing uproariously and writing down every single new word, as if they were cracking a code which had been impregnable for years, the rich white man's fancy language, always kept from them.

Gerald told me, 'you must get them to write something at every class,' but after our discussions, or rather yellings, we rarely got as far as that. Everyone joined in reading, discussing and shouting, while I often sat in silence, dumbfounded by the strange views I heard.

I never actually saw anyone in prison wearing a tinfoil hat to protect them against CIA mind-control radio waves, but a frustrating amount of time was spent listening to conspiracy theories, which all the prisoners from Poles to Afghan tribesmen seemed to embrace. Diana was murdered by the Royal Family, the Twin Towers were bombed by the Israelis, the CIA were behind the assassination of JFK, Scientologists run Hollywood, Jews control the world's money supply, AIDS was invented in a laboratory in Washington with the aim of wiping out black men, KFC deliberately sterilised black men, Robert Mugabe is a great African ruler, his reputation distorted by cunning white liars, and, of course, NASA faked the moon landings.

Partly, this addiction was based on sheer ignorance: one Geordie lad was astonished when I told him that the Soviet Union no longer existed; many people were bewildered because they didn't really have a clue where they were on the map . . . but the men seemed to need popular myths to justify their own failings. The thinking went along the lines of if everything is predetermined, with invisible forces, usually rich American capitalists controlling everything, I cannot be to blame for anything I have done.

It made them feel better, off the hook, to believe wild stories, but this idea of a planetary if not universal conspiracy also led to a feeling of generalised hopelessness. And some of it was rooted in truth. A Nigerian drug dealer listed Tony Blair, the Bhutto family and various African presidents as the most corrupt people in the world. 'They are all corrupt,' he said dismissively. 'They do very bad things then they move on to new jobs and do bad things again.'

If they can get away with it, he reasoned, why not him? The other men laughed when he said it, but I often heard similar views in prison: their own crime didn't count because bigger men were getting away with bigger things, and every system, everywhere, was corrupt.

I began to avoid key words which could unleash this tide of paranoia and words which had anything to do with religion.

There had once been a time, until about May 1989 when Iran issued a fatwa against Sir Salman Rushdie, that religion as a topic had been very quiet indeed. In the 1970s, when I first saw Tom Stoppard's play *Jumpers*, we all laughed when an unfortunate academic was offered a chair of Divinity.

'Not exactly in the eye of the storm, I know,' said his scheming boss. That joke is now entirely flat, almost inexplicable, like a one-liner from Shakespeare or an early Punch.

No one, not Enoch, nor Doris Stokes at her best, could have predicted that it would be religion not race or economics that would shatter any hope of peace among men, taking us back to an age of burnings and beheadings, where even the Archbishop of Canterbury would be reduced to the status of a useful idiot. As the globalised world shrank to fit itself inside Wormwood Scrubs, I could see Islam in the ascendant.

There was a short phase when I first started teaching in the Scrubs when so many of the inmates were Middle Eastern that some of my classes looked like a Saddam Hussein look-alike contest. Comfort was aghast when men in robes started praying in her classes. 'Suddenly I saw this backside sticking up,' she said, feeling affronted but helpless.

Sometimes they insisted on praying in the corridor, taking up a lot of room. Most of the Muslims disappeared from classes on Fridays. In the interests of 'diversity', they could do much as they liked, even wear their own clothing after sentence. We had one Muslim teacher on staff. He was civilised, smiling and friendly but now and then he would say things that jarred.

'I can't see why the separation of the sexes should be a problem,' he said one day.

An English IT teacher, who went round in cycling shorts and complained about people eating in the staffroom, agreed very strongly, adding that in a free society women should be free to be fully veiled. He obviously thought this was a clever idea, and I suspected he would really have been happier without seeing women around. The two men had the same idea, for different reasons.

Comfort was not happy with this discussion and as she listened she seemed to swell up to look even rounder than usual. 'Oh come off it, Yussuf,' she said, 'Just come off it.'

'Well, if that is what people choose for themselves, surely that is OK?' he said with the confident, reasonable smile of someone who thinks that he has seen the future and likes it.

His Arab evening class was so heavily subscribed that men could not get in the door. Even the Dutch drug-takers, mostly ageing former hippies, were attending. Only Narcotics Anonymous had more takers.

One day, an illiterate Irish lad who often cried in class and got beaten badly by the other prisoners for theft, appeared in my class wearing a full Moroccan *djellaba* and pointed shoes. I told him to go away and change, and he did. I wondered where this put me in terms of the FE mantra 'IAD at all times.'

Old men from the Karakoram and Hushe mountains of Pakistan sat in my classes in their Persian lamb hats, always seeming to pay great attention. I don't know if they were really interested, but they had a gentle courtesy that reminded me of my grandfather. Comfort, who came from the 'wake up and smell the cordite' persuasion, thought their polite attention was part of a hidden agenda, a deliberate plot to get to know the West the better to undermine it.

Others, even the fanatics, could not always be quite as Muslim as even they wanted to be. One day, as I came into the art room, Mahmud, a new student with a little pointed Ali Baba beard, was shouting out of the window at someone below. I told him to stop it.

'You are a racist!' he screamed, 'and you are against Islam.'

I toyed with the idea of saying something sarcastic but said nothing, and he ran out of the class slamming the doors. A short time later he ran back and just as suddenly got to work, painting diligently, standing at an easel copying a painting by Turner. I wanted to help him clean his brushes as he went along so the paint didn't get muddy, but he didn't want me to help him and seemed to want nothing to do with me.

I began to get very riled and considered saying, 'Look, I am the teacher here.' I didn't say it, and, at the end of the class, he thanked me for my offers of help. I was left wondering what his behaviour was all about – some of it was probably just down to anxiety.

In later classes, he expressed interest in the Impressionists and was smitten by a painting I showed him of some fat white roses by Henri Fantin-Latour. But later I heard him quietly giving advice to Vere, who, to my total surprise, turned out to be a Muslim convert.

He told him that he should not depict any living thing and that if he painted people or animals he should not put the eyes in, to stop them looking alive, or God would be 'offended'.

Vere, with his liking for Heather Mills look-alike lascivious angels, hummed and hawed about this, and I knew he would never tell me about it, as he could probably anticipate my reaction. He started missing classes, then came in and hung about listlessly. When I asked where he'd been, he explained that he wasn't sure that 'God wanted him to paint anymore.' I heard the word 'bollocks' slip out of my mouth as I just couldn't hold it in.

But as time went on I really liked Mahmud. He began to join in class discussions and became very jolly, except when the men lapsed into obscenities, and then he disapproved because I was there, which was nice for me. I was sad when he was suddenly deported back to Algeria, where he said he had no relations as they were now all in the UK. Like many Muslim prisoners, the last thing he wanted was to be deported to a Muslim country, where he was terrified of what would happen to him.

I suspected that if he had stayed in the UK he would have changed because in spite of himself he was passionately interested in Western art. I even imagined taking him to the National Gallery to look at Monet's paintings of the Thames. A friendship between us was unlikely but not impossible. Since then I have often wondered whether he looks back fondly on the rather crazy time he had with us, or if he is even still alive.

I also met a fanatical young man, detained for money-laundering in support of a terrorist group, who was writing a piece for *Free Time,* attacking US propaganda in the Arab world.

Small, quiet and charming, he told me that when he was younger – he must have meant about sixteen – he'd been sent by his London mosque to Chechnya where he saw the destitution caused by the Russian onslaught. After this experience, he had joined an extremist cell based in the mosque in Woolwich. He described how they sent groups of boys on 'holiday' to Syria where they would get into four-wheel-drive vehicles and make their way to Pakistan, then cross into Afghanistan to fight the British.

I wanted him to write about this experience for the magazine, but he was reluctant, as if it all had to be shrouded in secrecy. Fran discouraged him from talking about these things for his own good and because she distrusted the people ranged against him, but I could tell in my conversations with him that he wanted to write and that he was wavering in his commitment to Islamism.

His fanaticism had come from a group identity, which is so ferociously attractive to the young. Now he was in a different place with a very mixed group of people, including us in Education, and he liked us. We applauded his cleverness, made him feel special and asked him to analyse, write and express himself, which was also a very attractive proposition. Sadly, before I could find out anything further about him or gain his trust, he was whisked away to Top Security at Belmarsh. If he'd been left where he was he would have opened up a lot more.

Far removed from that boy, we also had quite a few London Islamo-chavs, who couldn't express themselves any more than their white counterparts and didn't want to write anything. They were fond of making grumpy remarks: 'I ain't doing none of this. I only want han Harabic education.'

'But don't you think it would be good to improve your English?'

'I dur' want no English.'

Walking through the dust ball of grime in the streets of East Acton, crossing the main arterial road where the M40 turns into the Marylebone flyover, I'd sometimes see their sisters, teetering on high stilettoes, wearing short, frilly smocks in bright colours over black leggings and head coverings. By some alchemy of religion and secularism, they managed to look extremely tarty and modest at the same time.

Many of the prisoners had never known anything but a strict Arab education. An Algerian in one of my lower English classes was very sunny and friendly, but when we had a discussion about myths he talked about Adam and Eve as if they were actual fact and revealed that he had never heard of evolution. I asked him about dinosaurs and how he thought they had existed, and what about the age of the Earth's rocks? But that was no good because he hadn't heard about either. I tried drawing dinosaurs on the whiteboard in case he recognised what they were, but I realised as I drew that I didn't know enough detail, what sort of feet they had, and they ended up looking like stuffed toys. All the men stared back at me blankly. I wondered what Muslim children in school would do if they were ever taken to the Natural History Museum and faced with the bony, skeletal evidence of life on Earth before the Garden of Eden.

The sunny Algerian adopted a sentimental approach towards the Old Testament, describing it as not just the literal truth about the origin of humankind but as the exact pattern for how we should live, revealing something about the Muslim obsession with shame.

'Adam and Eve were never naked,' he explained sweetly, as if talking to little children. 'God gave them both clothes right from the start made of leaves, because this is how men and women must be; it is as God made them.'

As a teenager, I enjoyed the fantasy of going back in time to meet people I admired such as Elizabeth I and Shakespeare. I imagined telling them about the future, how things had turned out. Now I was surprised to find how hard it is to talk to people who come from a different time, a distant age. I found that I just didn't have enough scientific facts to be able to present simple, logical arguments. I could not readily explain the combustion engine, electricity, microwaves or evolution. And the fact that they patently didn't believe anything I said was rather undermining. I feared that I often just sounded entrenched in my own culture.

The Algerian was happy to remain in God's enchanted playground where there were no measurable or controllable forces and the Almighty took care of everything, apart from sex, which was left to man to control fiercely.

One day in the library, sitting at a table of Muslims, who seemed to find me invisible, I heard a man, aged about thirty, say quite audibly and proudly, 'I have never had a woman you know. I am still a virgin.'

His friend, an English convert, replied, 'Well, you know, I deeply regret losing my virginity.' I doubt if those words had been heard within the prison before, even in the days of Queen Victoria.

I also found certain African attitudes perplexing and difficult to deal with. The old lie that Africans are not as intelligent as Westerners is patently wrong, but well-spoken, literate black men would start telling me about the 'danger of witches' and how 'demons often live in children and old people'.

In an attempt to look at this I held a class about the persecution of European witches in the seventeenth century, and we looked at the social and economic reasons why people made accusations of witchcraft. The men were not very responsive – it wasn't something that the Europeans usually worried about, and the Africans remained quiet. At the end, a student from Ghana told me that in his home village old people regularly turned themselves into balls of fire at night and entered people's homes to damage them.

I could have asked him for more details about what sort of 'damage' exactly they did and I wondered what happened to these old people, but I could see nothing I said would have any effect. I had no idea what to say to him. I started thinking that maybe I should take a GCSE in maths after all or perhaps go off and memorise the Periodic Table – anything to keep my grip on reason.

Yet, if being plunged in amongst this great mix of men was often mind-boggling, it was also exciting and exhausting.

At night, I continued going to parties for newspapers, my last toehold on my past career, and I sometimes regaled my classes the next day with my experiences, breaking the rule that said it was unwise to tell the men anything personal, in case they got some hold over us. I couldn't see the harm in it, and I wasn't afraid of them. If anything, I began to develop maternal feelings for them, and I could understand how teaching was once a popular career for single, childless women. They were often no more than children, and very childlike.

I liked to see their faces when I gave them glimpses of the outside: 'I was at a party last night,' I'd say, 'waiting for Peaches Geldof—'

'Oh were you, Miss? What's she like then? I like her,' or 'She's a real dog that one, ain't she?'

'Have you ever met that Kate Moss, Miss?'

'Have you ever met Salt-N-Pepa? Foxy Brown? Ever met Eve?'

The answer was no, and I usually didn't know who they were talking about, but then I didn't always recognise the ones I was supposed to be spotting either.

I enjoyed telling them stories about some of my adventures – but not all of them, and any bitterness about my life I left at the gate. Like POWs, we were duty-bound to keep each other going with stories and jokes. This wasn't difficult as the men could be so entertaining and coming to Education was their small chance to shine.

6

A large London prison is something like a cross between a monastery and a prison camp. Arrival through the mighty historic gates and then the first three months of adjustment are the worst. Prisoner WJ, addicted to heroin or 'Miss Brown' as he called it, described it in a poem:

> *You're inside now bruv, this is your new home,*
> *'You got the top bunk mate,' 'Oh shit,' I hear you*
>   *moan*
> *Your kit is a pillow case, you start to unpack*
> *Regrets overwhelm you, Time, you can't turn back*
> *Get on with your bird keep your head down*
> *Think of what put you here, that nasty Miss Brown.*

'I've got a new cellmate, and he cries all night,' one man told me. 'He was a solicitor, and he isn't used to places like this.'

Arriving in the reception wing, all prisoners have to share a cell with a stranger. Some of the East European lads choose to be together, but most people prefer to be alone, or at least to have the choice, but that is a privilege only available after they have been inside for some time.

One prisoner, calling himself, 'Sage of Imam', wrote a poem, called 'First Night's Discovery', which began:

*Do not be shocked with your new home. Relax and
    enter.*
*Be in it, yet out of it. Do not allow your mind to trap
    you in here.*
*Let it remain free like a bird. Remain composed and
    patient.*
Do not get frustrated or allow yourself to be afraid.

Sooner said than done. 'I've got scars upon my heart, Miss,' said Peter, 'from having to share a cell.'

He had a gentle manner and looked very grave as he remembered his early days in the Scrubs, and I wondered what he had been through.

'I was in with this older brother,' he said, meaning another Afro-Caribbean, 'and it was terrible, the worst experience of my life.'

The whole class was agog. I thought, it must have been a terrible trauma, what he must have been through!

'He kept farting. It was unbearable.'

Not exactly what I had expected, but he pressed on, looking intense.

'There was no escape from it. All night I'd hide under my blanket, but it was like a hurricane blowing through the cell. I had to keep rushing to the bars to try to breathe, I couldn't get away from it. And the lavatory, it had no door, it was open. Have you ever had to sit in a small room while an adult man passes a motion in front of you, Miss?'

Well, he had obviously paid a high price for diddling a building society. I got an image of his cellmate as a grizzled old black man who was not really aware of the effect he had on others.

'He had the most terrible stinking feet too,' said Peter, while all the men reeled about laughing, 'and he put them up on the table every time I started eating.'

He'd suffered this for a month before he was allowed to move to another cell.

Smelly or not, cellmates rely on each other, and finding a good one matters much more than a good flatmate. One prisoner wrote a poem about this called 'Mackerel Fishing'.

> I'm going mackerel fishing my cellmate free to roam;
> I'm glad he's got his freedom but
> Now I'm on my own.
> I'm going mackerel fishing I wouldn't mind a sprat
> Because I don't want to wear my teabags like a
>   bloody hat.
> I'm going mackerel fishing
> I'll have to set some traps.[. . .]
> I'm going mackerel fishing I hope he's not too big;
> I don't want my burn stuffed down my knickers
> And my stamps stuck to my bum.[. . .]
> Hope I don't get a cod because I'll throw
> Him back in the water
> If I catch him playing with his knob.
> I'm going mackerel fishing for the cellmate of my
>   dreams
> But I'll choke the little guppy
> If I catch him in my jeans.

Men could be moved immediately if a cellmate was violent. I never heard of anyone suffering sexual abuse from another inmate. The cult of rape in prison is a colourful myth, vividly illustrated in David Mamet's play Edmond. In this modern American Rake's Progress, set in the 1980s, Edmond, a white middle-class man in his mid-thirties, gets into bad company and, in Scene 20, ends up in a prison cell with 'a large, black prisoner'. There is a horrible atmosphere of menace as Edmond makes conversation in his educated highfalutin' way, coming to a halt when his new cellmate says, 'I think you should just get on my body.' A rape scene follows.

Those words sum up the average non-convict's nightmare. But this myth ignores the fact that most of the black men who fill British gaols detest sodomy. Homophobia in prison is so strong that I suggested we should get gay-rights campaigner Peter Tatchell to come in and talk to the men in one of their combative 'Skills for Life' sessions. The Governor refused, saying Tatchell would not be safe. When it was pointed out that he could handle almost anything, having taken on the forces of Robert Mugabe, Vladimir Putin and two Archbishops of Canterbury, the Governor said he could not enter the prison as it would cause a riot of protest.

There may be a cruel cult of rape in US gaols, but it hasn't come here. Whatever power games go on in English prisons, they are not expressed through sexual violence.

'It doesn't happen here, because this place is so English,' a Greek teacher said to me. I wasn't quite sure what she meant, but I think it had something to do with a certain reticence. I once saw a man in a wheelchair lose his sweatpants slightly as he struggled to move to a chair. All the men around him looked away quickly. One of them told me he was reluctant to go to the showers because they are all open to view. I suggested that he should go along with a friend. He was shocked.

'I can't do that, Miss,' he said. 'Men don't do that sort of thing.' The idea of doing anything that might give the slightest hint of gayness was out of the question.

Inmates did not talk about sex, never discussed their girl-friends, never gave the impression of being avid for hard-core pornography, and young girls in the office who wore short skirts incurred disapproval. It was as if they didn't want to be teased and bothered by things they could not have. From what we saw in Education, 'doing bird', at least in the Scrubs, meant keeping the lid on. Repression we can still do.

After a few weeks inside, people make friends and adapt to their new life, as I had done too. Once you get to know people it is possible to sink into an intense protective cama-raderie such as you've probably never experienced, unless you've been in the Army or have been caught up in a major disaster. Men whose lives have hit a wall unite in their griev-ances, annoyances and the sheer struggle to get by.

There are many former robbers among them, and they are all robbed by the 'System', particularly the in-house 'pin phone' system. An article in *The Guardian* (2 April 2007) showed that inmates were forced to pay up to five times more for using this than for a comparative call using a BT public payphone. BT charged 30p for a fifteen-minute phone call, but it was £1.65 for the same call from prison.

There was a case for saying phone calls in prison could have been made cheaper, because of bulk use, with long queues of men waiting every evening for a chance to use a phone. Waiting in that line, they knew more certainly than at any other time that they were truly a captive audience.

Peter and Hardip told me about a case where one inmate had challenged BT for this policy. The Ombudsman found that in a two-month period he had paid £70.08 for calls that would have cost £15.20 from a payphone outside. They also came up with the surprising fact that the Prison Service receives a 10-per-cent commission from BT on inmates' phone credits. Salt, pepper, toilet paper, washing things and toothpaste are also overpriced in prison, and there is a precious 50p a week charged for use of a TV.

The other major cause of discontent inside is the food. Most cons would be satisfied with a diet of chicken, rice, sweet potatoes and peas, with fruit to follow, but they get overcooked slop brought in from outside, reheated and bunged at them in cardboard containers, a grim parody of McDonald's.

They eat in their cells, which get smelly and clogged with debris, some of which gets thrown out onto the pathway below. A refectory, which they used to have until the 1970s, would be more civilised – could even be a place for creativity – and would be less lonely, but that would take much more organising, more staff and more security, so it can't happen.

On canteen night they can buy food and try to cook it themselves in their cells. They do this by boiling food in plastic bags in their kettles. They also heat oily tinned fish on the element. This doesn't make the tea taste good and is a punishable offence, but it is a tiny bit of domesticity and, if the cell is shared, the nearest you get to a dinner party.

There are so many cookery books around, but as far as I know no one has yet come up with *The Prison Kettle Cookery Book*, written for a couple with a joint income of £23.60 a week before expenses. I would challenge any celebrity chef to do it.

The main privations in prison are of course sex and drink. They can fantasise about one, but the other takes initiative.

> *Wormwood Scrubs Punch* (40 per cent proof on a good day): Collect as many apples, pears or oranges you can. Soak brown bread in warm water, discard

bread and water, yeast gathers at the bottom. Ferment sugar, yeast, water and fruit for seven days. Consume immediately or hide beverage under your bunk. Penalty for use: one week on the punishment block.

Many also resent the prison's dirty neglectedness. They call the Scrubs a 'hovel'. It is some consolation to know that according to rumour Pentonville Prison is worse, but looking at the litter, the thick dust and unswept stairways, there is always a sense that inmates have been thrown on a huge urban rubbish heap.

Despite press stories about prisoners living in luxury, going to prison is not good for your health. Some men spend a lot of time in the gym pumping up their muscles, but if they are ill they get very poor treatment. There is particular contempt for the mainly Nigerian medical staff. The prisoners hated them, and it seemed reciprocal.

This problem possibly comes from cultural differences which mean that the Nigerians tend to see the prisoners as people worthy only of continual punishment in deep dark cells. I heard an African doctor shout at an inmate who had waited patiently for attention: 'You are a prisoner! Why are you coming here making demands?'

I had a prisoner in a class who was taken ill, the side of his face swelling alarmingly. I thought he had an allergic reaction to something and asked the guard to get a nurse. The Nigerian nurse duly waddled in, her own face also pumped up, inflated with indignation. She looked at the prisoner from the doorway before declaring, 'He can wait till he goes back to the wing to see me there.'

As she left, I saw the prisoner's eyes roll back as if he was going to faint, and I told him to put his head on his arms and just try to rest until the end of the class, another hour and a half. I shudder to think how she would have treated a man having a breakdown.

A lot of men were in prison because they were just greedy and unlucky, but many others were there because they were mentally ill. Many of them needed a psychotherapist, and without psychiatric help they could never really settle down enough to learn anything. As Charley the mischievous IT teacher put it, 'They should do away with the Education Department altogether and replace it with intensive therapy.'

Prison is bad, 'the hovel' everyone agrees, but life for some people is worse outside. One afternoon in the library, a boy whom I didn't know kept trying to attract my attention. I was scanning the newspapers, which always arrived several days late, adding to the feeling of being abroad, cut off in a strange land. I didn't want to be disturbed, which made him pester me more. After quite a lot of banter, he told me in a whisper that his name was Terry and that he was worried about his legs.

Pale, and so thin that he looked almost transparent, he showed me that he was wearing four pairs of grey tracksuit bottoms to try to bulk them out.

'They are disintegrating,' he told me seriously. 'They are like glass. I worry so I can't eat, then me legs get all thin and I think they will break if I knock them or someone knocks into me. I can't go to the gym and I stay in me cell most of the time.'

I finally put down my paper to listen. He told me his fear of disintegrating bones often dominated his whole life. It came and went, but he was entering a period of intense anxiety. It reminded me of the case of Charles VI, King of France in the fourteenth century, known as 'Charles the

Mad', who believed he was made of glass and was terrified of being touched.

Terry had been brought up in East London and described a happy home life, but things changed when he was eleven after his father found him a Saturday job on a stall in Romford Market. He was buggered by the stall owner for the next four years. He eventually told his father, who tried to kill the offender. The police got involved, and the abuser was sent to prison. The whole thing became a taboo subject at home, never discussed, and he received no help. After that, his life went awry: he dropped out of school, got into petty crime and violence, and, by the age of twenty-four, he was on his sixth custodial sentence.

I told him that when he left prison he should try to get some long-term psychotherapy as there is none available inside. This was a bit like telling a vagrant he could cheer himself up by taking a skiing holiday or having a look at the Piero in the National Gallery. I didn't think therapy would be in his frame of reference at all, but I couldn't think of anything else to suggest.

I was pleased to see that he did understand what I meant. He mentioned a family doctor, unfortunately now retired, who had taken an interest in him in the past. He understood that he was suffering and could be helped, but it seemed that he had no real sense that he deserved anything. He felt bad and worthless. He had lost contact with his family, had few friends, no job prospects and no life on the outside.

Terry seemed so helpless and frail that I couldn't understand how he survived on the outside. I asked him if he perhaps preferred being inside?

'Are you fucking mad?' he said, laughing. Then he said, 'Out there, my life is all over the place. I've got no job, I don't get on with my family, there is drugs and crime, but in here you get a lot of order. Everything is worked out for you. I do like that.'

A London prison is a small town, where there is almost no private physical experience and no part of the day or night that is entirely unsupervised. A second chance at infancy, prison provided the all-embracing care Terry had never had. But it was also about stasis: nothing going wrong, nothing right, no development. Eventually, he would just be tipped out onto the street with £40 in his pocket and left to hobble away on his dissolving legs.

Like photocopiers and lavatories, therapists were rare in prison – perhaps I should say 'as rare as teeth'. I always found it odd to see so many men walking round with rotten teeth or often no teeth at all. I hadn't seen that since I lived in Communist Poland. The diet doesn't help, but the dentistry available is almost non-existent.

David arrived in the art room, with greyish-green skin and a mouthful of rotting teeth. Like many of the inmates, unable to see a dentist, he was permanently on painkillers. Of course, many of them didn't like the dentist, but in the Scrubs the feeling was reciprocal. At one time, the dentist's chair was broken and remained unmended and unused for three months.

In my art class, David with the bad teeth told me he was in for burning down his girlfriend's house while she and their baby were still in it. They had escaped, but he was now considered dangerous to women.

'Women are usually the problem,' he told me with a grisly smile. I made a mental note to always be gentle with him.

There had been other incidents when he had been aggressive towards women, so he was now on an 'indeterminate sentence', a sentencing system brought in under the Criminal Justice Act of 2003, which the prisoners feared as it meant they could be kept in for years until they could prove that they were safe to release. It also meant a life on licence, always with the threat of being hauled back inside.

David, usually sitting with his head hanging down, was unlikely ever to prove anything. He was on anti-psychotic drugs, which seemed to shut him off from other people.

'It's not right, Miss,' he'd say. 'They have a really bad effect on me.'

He was socially and emotionally crippled by his condition and knew it, but he seemed to gain a bit from the company he found in the art room and from my interest. In the brief periods that he could concentrate he loved painting from photos of wild animals. He copied a photo of some elephants, and it worked well. He grasped the idea of tone and liked working them out from old black and white photos. When he saw he could make an effective painting, he became enthusiastic for more art work.

I suggested he should give some of the paintings to his mother on her visits to take home and keep safely for him. I thought she might like to have them herself. 'She wouldn't be interested,' he said, and I felt his whole rotten childhood banked up behind those words.

As he got more interested in painting, he talked about going to Harrow College one day to take a foundation course. The college with the prison contract claims in its 'mission statement' that 'Art is seen as constructive use of the prisoners' time, encouraging their educational ambitions,' but which college would take a man like David? Which society? Like Terry, he was happier in prison, or at least in some kind of closed society.

'It's the only place where I have ever had any help,' he said. 'This is the only place where anyone has ever been interested in me.'

The prison rattled on, like an unstoppable old train, always on the point of breaking down and always full to bursting. Men occupied themselves by gossiping, complaining, cooking food in their kettles. Some became passive and bored; others got too frustrated and were carted off to 'the block' – the punishment cells – or to the Mary Seacole Centre if they became seriously deranged.

Foch, a beautiful young man with black doe eyes, who had once been a child model, returned from a spell on the block looking very lean and healthy as if he'd been to a spa.

'A change is as good as a rest, Miss,' he said, winking at me, before breaking into a wild impromptu dance which suggested he was quite glad to get out of there.

Typical of the topsy-turvy nature of prison, many men claimed that conditions were better on the block than the normal wings: better food and more chances to wash and get clean clothes.

Wherever they were in the prison, men got bedded down and settled. Some would barricade themselves in their cells rather than face being moved to another prison, perhaps because they had an enemy there or because they just didn't want to be moved on suddenly, from one uprooted town to the next.

A drug dealer from Dublin, who had been living in a caravan in North Wales, went on a dirty protest when he was due to be removed. He said his lavatory was already blocked so he just smashed it open. His cell filled up, and he decorated the walls and himself with excrement.

One spring morning, I heard a voice shouting my name. He was calling me from his punishment cell on 'the block'. He stuck a long, tattooed arm through the grilles and waved wildly to me, beckoning me to come across the wide yard and talk to him. I wanted to shout over and give him a bit of encouragement, have a bit of banter, but instantly there was the feeling of being watched, that I would be breaking some rule if I did. In prison, all normal relations between people are distorted or strained. So I waved from a distance and walked on.

When he visited us in the art room, hosed down, shaved head shining, he told me that the SERCO van drivers wouldn't take him to another prison because he'd been on a dirty protest as they were too worried that he might continue the protest in the van.

'I would have done it, oh yes,' he said, his eyes glittering coldly. 'I'd have made a real mess in the van.' He seemed to have gone back to being a helpless child raging at the forces against him.

Sometimes I heard talk about suicides and beatings. Low-level, sporadic violence was part of life on the wings – some wings more notorious than others. This came from lack of communication, frustration and boredom and from too many unhappy men being banged up for most of the time with no one they could trust to help them.

A Vietnamese youth, who'd been arrested after a fight, thought he was in for selling pirated DVDs. No one could find an interpreter to tell him the real situation. When he found out that the charge against him was murder, he hanged himself. The officer who told me about this, who had found his body hanging from a towel attached to the side of his bunk bed, was nonchalant about it. There were so many suicides, sometimes two a day, always by hanging. 'They are ingenious about it,' he said.

One man managed to hang himself even though he had a cellmate. He used a towel and jumped from his top bunk. The prisoner sleeping below found him in the morning and was traumatised.

I heard from several different men about a prisoner who was badly beaten by the officers on his wing. Abdul Nadjibulla, who weighed about thirty stone, was the fattest man I'd ever seen, that any of us had ever seen. A year after he'd left the Scrubs, I still heard people exclaim, 'He was the fattest man I've ever seen!'

When I first saw him in one of my English classes my heart sank as he just looked too awful. He gazed back at me apprehensively from inside his fatty hideout. 'A big lad you got in there,' said an officer passing by, loudly enough for everyone to hear.

Abdul looked like an African American, perhaps because he was dressed in US baseball strip, complete with cap. I could see him on the touchline at a baseball game, stuffing himself with popcorn and cola – the fat character in a comic film, except he wasn't comical at all, and he could no longer walk as his knees had given out. He had an African accent, but his lungs were so compressed by fat that he couldn't speak above a whisper.

Nothing about him seemed to make sense. He'd grown up in Liberia during the vicious civil war when his fellow countrymen were maiming each other. He got a good chance for something better when he was sent to the University in Kiev to train as a doctor. But in his fifth year at medical school, for some reason, he had come to London and had committed a violent robbery in Wembley. I know London is a magnet for robbers of every description from all round the globe, but what kind of street robber weighs thirty stones and is confined to a special wheelchair? When the police arrested him they found a stun gun in his car, which he said he needed, 'to defend himself in Wembley'.

'He drives a car?' was usually the surprised response to this information. He had made a rough sketch of himself being dragged out of the car by police. As they struggled to extract him he had suffered crush injuries to his chest, and he wanted to sue them. He asked me to copy these drawings for him to show in court, but I just couldn't bring myself to do it as it seemed so grotesque and I couldn't believe he would get anywhere with the case.

His wheelchair was too wide for the classroom entrance, so he would rise out of it with the aid of an officer and a helper, then waddle and lunge forwards, catching hold of the edge of the desk, before lowering himself into two seats.

When I got used to his constant wheezing and the voice so quiet that we could hardly hear him read, I liked having him in my class. He seemed to have a humane, reasoning mind. He could never get to the library as the only lift was too far from his wing, so I borrowed books for him.

When we watched films on a Friday afternoon, he would be upset at any scenes of violence. We once watched *Missing*, the 1982 film by Costa-Gavras, about the Pinochet coup in Chile. When we came to the scene where the hero of the film, played by Jack Lemmon, looks up and sees endless naked bodies scattered on a glass roof above him, I saw Abdul put his head down, cover his face with his hands and give a long sigh.

What he liked best was taking exams. He got through as many as possible – the way other people do crosswords in the tabloids. Once, invigilating, in a Level One Maths exam, I sat at the end of the room facing his huge panting back watching how he concentrated. This was the kind of maths he would have mastered as a small boy, but he took it very seriously, enjoying every minute I think, and he asked me to call out when he had half an hour left, then fifteen minutes, as if was a crucial test. He was almost immobile, like a great grub, but his mind was still desperately flexible, longing for something to do.

During the three months I knew him he never lost any of the weight, which was clearly killing him. If anything, he gained it. 'The diet sheet they've given me doesn't work,' he said sadly. His condition was obviously way beyond the Scrubs medical centre with its bracing 'pull your socks up and be grateful' attitude.

Eventually he went to court and was released but immediately rearrested at the gate. This was one of the worst fates for a prisoner, at least those who want to get out, who have a life to go to. While they've been inside, the police gather evidence about some other crime, and when the prisoner reaches the main gate they seize them for that. This situation often breaks a prisoner.

Abdul was just one of millions of mysterious globalised travellers, often traumatised by violence, who travel the world looking for a better life but bring the disaster of their past with them. I don't know what he did to provoke people but I heard that one night on the wing he annoyed the officer on duty, and then other officers got involved. I was told that all the other prisoners were sent back to their cells and locked in, but Abdul was dragged out.

'I could see him lying on the ground bleeding,' a prisoner told me.

'We could all hear him wailing,' said another. No one could tell me exactly why this had happened, or where Abdul was now. I never saw him in Education again, but I often wondered how he came to rob someone and how that vast body ended up on the ground outside his cell covered in blood.

It was the kind of scene that we women teachers in Education could not really imagine, the life led by the men on the wings.

Just before Christmas, Isaac was released, without the chance to say goodbye to anyone. Suddenly he was gone. It had echoes of the concentration camp, where people suddenly disappear into the void without a word. We were all saddened, and I wondered if such a disregard for human feeling did the prisoners any good. To my mind it made them more cynical and alienated. Being moved without warning is part of prison life. Perhaps it appeals to the public's idea of punishment, but this lack of autonomy was also part of the infantilising process.

Old Frank was moved to another prison, but not the lower category he longed for. His murals were nearly complete but he still hadn't received the varnish, so he had to leave without finishing. I heard that when he was told he had to go he cried a lot.

Christmas in prison is not like anywhere else, except perhaps Tehran or Pyongyang. Men are separated from their families. Many are far from home, and, apart from a religious service on the day, all festivity has been abolished.

There is no special Christmas food except for a small amount of chocolate if they go to a church service. They prepare food in their kettles and may be alone as there are too few officers on duty to organise any 'association'.

But, of course, Christmas arrives with people who bring it in with them on their shoes, in their pockets and on their faces. Even if you work in a prison it is almost impossible not to respond to the season, not to behave differently and to expect other people to do the same.

I took in homemade mince pies and some good quality M&S biscuits. I put them on the table in the art room in an old unglazed coil pot and watched them disappear, keeping a tin ready for hiding them if anyone from Security looked round the door.

The remaining hostile clique emerged from behind their protective sheets. Even Martin, who had never spoken to me, could not resist this gift from the non-music-loving whitey. I saw his long elegant fingers crawl slowly towards the extra chocolatey orange bics. I commented on his love of biscuits, and he almost smiled at me, but not quite. I decided, with the Christmas spirit in me, that he did quite like me but was extraordinarily shy.

On the last afternoon before the Christmas lockdown, Rodriguez, a prisoner from Colombia, who wore long thick braids in a bright bandana, brought in a tray of tea and biscuits. No one knew where he got them, but it was probably a gesture from the officer who was there that day – a little spontaneous gesture of kindness.

I agree with C. G. Gardiner, who was in charge of setting up workers' canteens in London during the Second World War, when he wrote that 'psychologically, tea breeds contentment. It is so bound up with fellowship and the home and pleasant memories that its results are almost magic.'

He was right, and it certainly worked in the Scrubs. There was suddenly such a good mood that even Ben sat smiling benignly, although he might have had a joint somewhere.

Bill served out the tea, but when he went away for a few moments the men began joshing me rather coyly:

'Haven't you noticed anything?'

'Bill only comes to these classes because of you.'

'He's mad about you.'

'I wish we had some real coffee instead of teabags,' I moaned as Bill returned.

'Get the coffee on for the lady, Bill,' they called, somehow summoning up, despite the bleakness of the room, the image of a cosy domestic scene between the two of us.

On a cold day, in the sparse, dirty room, they had conjured up the image of quiet, private home life, and it seemed to hang in the air before all of us, a ghost in the room, the spirit of what Charlotte Brontë once called 'loving simplicity', that ideal peace between a couple as they go about ordinary activities together. For a moment it was there before us gleaming like fancy lights, then we all started joking and it flickered away.

Everyone was amused, including Bill. It was all so good-natured that it wasn't embarrassing, although Bill and I didn't look at each other so much after that.

As it was Christmas, the teachers were invited to the Officers' Club, a bar and billiard room in what looked like a brick outhouse just outside the visitors' entrance to the prison. Inside it was dark and dingy, perhaps due to the layers of nicotine on the walls and ceiling. The gloom was lit up by flashes from fruit machines and a giant TV screen revealing a vast flag of St George on the wall behind the bar.

Such is the divide between officers and teachers that only Fran, Marjorie and I went along, out of curiosity. I felt relieved that Marjorie had decided to be very friendly, and we chatted like old pals while enormous men in white shirts containing guts the size of beer barrels, girdled with shining key chains, lumbered in shouting: 'Alright, Son?' to each other.

Mr Zippo sat at a small round table, looking a little less defensive and stern than usual, surrounded by large female officers with ponytails. There was an aura of sex around them and I was rather impressed at how their stout legs balanced on high stilettos, glistened as they emerged from tight pencil skirts, and the stylish way they let their thick black belts and chains dangle. Many an Englishman's dream.

In a back room I saw sporting cups and trophies and a very long black and white photograph of the prison staff taken in 1931. They looked paler and more malnourished than now; a line of whey-faced, bitter-looking men, with narrow eyes, some sporting Hitler moustaches. They could have been former workhouse boys, perhaps brutalised by the 1914–18 conflict and the war in Ireland.

I often long for imaginary pasts but I shuddered at the image of these people, not tempted to go back to their time at all. Yet the culture hadn't changed that much as we teachers were just as divided from the present-day prison officers, by class and culture, as we would have been from the men in the photo.

Someone pointed out the actual, 'Number One Guv'nor' himself, standing at the bar. Fran and I approached him, smiling cautiously, hoping to have a productive talk. He had come up through the ranks, starting as an officer, or warder as they were known then. He rather resembled an Old Labour MP, grizzled and rotund, a former docker or ship's steward, someone not afraid of a fistfight.

He was fairly amiable but didn't say much and, while he half listened, he looked over at the bottles behind the bar or at the barmaid and smiled at her. Having a Christmas drink with the staff was one thing but talking to teachers was quite another. We smiled politely and beat a retreat.

Just before the Christmas break I finally got a reply from him, via Kantila, saying that Tony Benn would not be allowed into the prison. No reason was given. This was embarrassing as I had kept Benn waiting for weeks for a date in his over-busy diary when he could do it. He took the rejection philosophically, and I hoped he felt proud to think that someone still saw him as being so dangerous.

At New Year, while the prison was still locked down for the holiday, John organised a group of us to set about cleaning and painting the art room. This was only possible because the same generous officer who had given us tea also decided to bring paint and rollers in from home, and he supplied some overalls.

It was all unofficial and felt very exciting. Bill bossed everyone about and behaved as if he'd been a painter and decorator all his life. We plastered white on the walls and blue on windows and pipes. Everyone in the art classes was invited to take part.

'I ain't doing nothing for this prison,' said Martin bitterly, speaking to me for the first time.

Ben turned up but only to hang about aimlessly, firing staples at passers-by. He was in a bad way, as he had been due to be deported to Jamaica a month earlier and was still waiting. He had spent Christmas inside even though he was technically a free man. He was one of many prisoners left stranded by the immigration service. Like Ben, they are neither released nor deported, with no reason given, which drives them crazy – and the people who have to look after them.

In 2006, over 1,000 dangerous prisoners were released by mistake when they were due for deportation, but a lot of men do not get released or deported, even when they have finished their sentences. This is because papers are lost, because the country they are going to doesn't want them, or because they have already been deported from one country and have claimed asylum at Heathrow and their true nationality is not known.

'What are you going to do today?' I asked Ben when classes started again.

'Fuck all,' he replied succinctly.

We were still clearing out the clutter from the room, and I asked him to sort out work he wanted to keep from stuff he could throw away. He refused. I asked him several times, then warned him that anything looking like rubbish would go in the bin unless he wanted it. He wouldn't come over and look so I put some of his stuff into the bin. He became enraged, shouting 'blood clat' and bawling abuse at me.

'Don't fuck with me,' he shouted.

'Don't fuck with me,' I screamed back.

This was dangerous: things were escalating, so I warned him that I would press the alarm if he went on being so threatening. He stopped immediately as, despite what the key man had said, the green buttons were hardly ever touched.

'Threatening?' he said, surprised. 'I'm not threatenin' no wo-man.'

He couldn't see how he looked from where I stood.

'You are treating me like a prisoner,' he said hopelessly, subsiding into a heap.

He had a point. His sentence was over, but he was still inside, an impossible situation for all of us, and I had no idea how to get him to cooperate. Eventually, a very large black woman teacher came in and threatened him with a stick. This parody of childhood discipline helped for a while. He could take that kind of thing from her. We all laughed, and he had got a bit of special attention.

We had another month of his listless destructiveness before he was gone. We all felt relief when it finally happened but Martin began hanging around after class, as if he didn't want to go back to his cell.

'You must be missing Ben,' I said.

'No.' he said. 'Men don't miss men.'

So there I had it, one of the rules of his culture, unknown to me.

He was released not long after, along with Vere. Isaac came back as suddenly as he went, for the burglary of a warehouse. He'd broken in looking for somewhere to sleep after taking heroin.

Rupert, still working on his Flayed Angel, was suddenly moved for his own safety after it got out that he was inside for rape.

With Ben and Martin gone, their clique finally broke up. More men came in, including Tony Ten Boom, a big Dutchman who just strolled over one day, turned the rap music off and put on some light classical stuff that suited him.

Perhaps because he was large or just because he smiled so winningly, no one argued with him. With that, the whole atmosphere in the room lightened. John's long-held plans for changes in the art room were happening, and I realised that in this district of London called the Scrubs nothing changes but nothing remains the same for long.

7

Observations are now constant throughout education, training and teaching, a bit like having to take a driving test three or four times a year, and, despite union objections, they can be used for getting rid of teachers who don't come up to scratch under scrutiny.

I remember hearing about this ordeal when I was a university student from friends who were wisely, as things turned out, taking their PGCE along with their first degree or taking a combined honours with Education. I had no plans to be a teacher and listened with detachment to their descriptions of disasters under observation: PE equipment taking so long to put out that the lesson was ending before it had been used; a lesson on weights and measures in which a small boy got sand in his grommet; slide projectors that suddenly wouldn't work or slides constantly appearing upside down. Now I shuddered at the thought of it – a critical person in the corner of the room, watching me struggle with a class.

Being observed in prison is a rigmarole. I put in an application for a visitor to the prison, and they had to get security clearance. I had to find someone to escort me to collect the tutor from the main entrance and then back again to Education, at a time when most teachers would be rushing to their classrooms. I knew that if he was late and classes had started I wouldn't be able to find anyone to do it.

Apart from worrying about that, I had to prepare a class that would impress the tutor. I thought I'd use the Friday group and have a go at teaching simile and metaphor and perhaps extended metaphor. Simple enough, and it could be fun: I would start by comparing metaphor to simile: A is B. You are my sunshine. The Lord is my Shepherd. Then, your eyes are like the sun, her hair is like a worm's wedding, a woman without a man is like a fish without a bicycle.

I would take it a bit further by discussing the imagery in a short modern poem called 'Incendiary' by Vernon Scannell, about an abused boy who takes to arson. Then I would plunge into more serious literature, look at our most famous extended metaphor, the speech beginning 'All the world's a stage', from *As You Like It*. I would end by getting them to compose metaphors of their own.

I would be examined on my planning and preparation, selection and use of materials, learning and teaching methods, group management and class atmosphere. There was also a section on 'assessment and record keeping'.

There was nowhere in the Scrubs to get colour printing or enlargements done, so I had to go into the back streets of Shepherd's Bush to a small printing business to get some snazzy photocopies from an old illustrated *Complete Works*.

I got my materials sorted, found a tutor to come out on a Friday and told the men what would be happening. They didn't show much interest but I was pretty sure they would behave well, as the group was so good-natured.

At 8.30 a.m. on the day I could see Jeff in the distant outer chamber, looking a bit anxious. He was unnerved by the place, and we walked up to Education in silence. This was reassuring as I felt horribly nervous about being observed. As we started the class, I knew I was talking too fast. I tried to slow things down and concentrate on 'inclusiveness', making sure each man was involved. At one point, I lost track of what I was doing. Things swam before my eyes, then I pulled myself together and, about halfway through, suddenly had a feeling of intense relief: it was going well and probably nothing would go wrong. The men had all behaved perfectly.

At the end of the class, Jeff smiled with satisfaction and, I think, relief, as if his own ordeal was over. He complimented me on my beautiful photocopies. I thought it was really good of him to notice a detail like that.

'I'd quite like to work here too,' he said as he left, looking happy it was safely over.

In his 'summative comments' on my observation, he said the class had been excellent, one of the best he had observed in a long time. In his 'areas for development', he mentioned that I needed to expand my scheme of work, a forward plan for about a month of classes, and pay more attention to each prisoner's 'individual learning programme', which had to be filled in some time during each class. He'd spotted, of course, that I wasn't keen on paperwork, and no one could get away with that. But things were going well.

Fran suggested I should apply for the permanent job of 'literacy tutor', which was about to be advertised in the press. This was my first-ever serious encounter with job-application forms. In the distant past I'd written letters to provincial newspaper editors, and when I arrived in London I'd rung up St Thomas' Hospital offering my services as a bath attendant after hearing from a retired nurse at Morley College that auxillaries were always needed. I was told I'd have to have two interviews for the job, but when they started measuring me for the nylon uniform during the first one I knew I was in with a chance. I'd only fallen into jobs or snatched them easily.

The form for the literacy job stretched for ten pages. The listed qualifications had changed since I was a student; subjects had even changed their names. Plain old History was now listed as 'History and Classical Civilisation'. Instead of spaces to list three A-level results, there were gaps for up to ten. The exam grades were embarrassing. My two starred As now looked like nothing, and my good old 2.2 looked bad. I couldn't see any mention of Thirds, once so prized by brilliant bad boys.

There was also an amazing list of other requirements. To teach literacy I had to be capable of no less than sixteen 'main duties', eight 'personal skills' and five areas of 'qualification and experience'. It was a baffling list.

Gerald told me that the actual definition of most jobs has changed, become more vague, so that people are expected to be able to do a bit of everything. If everyone can do everything you can cut your work force in half, and no one is ever left idle, always filling in for other people. If a teacher applies for a job in a museum education department, they might not be asked if they are interested in history, but they will be expected to have a degree, teaching experience, a second language (preferably Punjabi or Polish), with call-centre, cash-handling and retail experience marked as 'desirable'. Cleaning and maintenance may also be thrown in.

I decided to ignore all that and to write a short essay trying to minimise journalism and emphasise teaching experience. I twisted and stretched the facts like someone making a sausage dog out of balloons, but I'd still only got teaching in Poland for a year in the 1970s and a TEFL course from the 1980s (for which I only scraped a grade C). All I had in my favour was my current teaching course and my prison work, and my favourable observation reports. I was doing the job I was applying for, but I didn't get shortlisted.

'Your application form was shit,' said Fran, looking exasperated. 'Why didn't you apply properly? She had no idea how unaccustomed I was to this world of ordinary work. 'You must tick all the boxes,' she told me. I must still have looked blank because she explained that I needed to answer point by point, filling in each separate criteria. It was dreadfully dull, but there was no other way. The age of the essay was over.

Comfort also wanted the job, and I was told on the quiet that Kantila wanted her for the job and had coached her on completing the form. She had been in the prison for over a year with her own designated classroom so it seemed fair that she should get it. I didn't want to tread on toes – not hers anyway, as I really liked her. I had no driving ambition, not really taking things too seriously, still not really believing that this was my new reality.

'Think about yourself and what you want, not about Comfort,' Fran said. But I wasn't sure what I wanted, and Comfort was sure she wanted that job.

Fran was worried that the college would bring in someone of their own.

'It has got to be you or Comfort,' she said, with real anxiety. 'I know you can both work well here, and I don't want my team to be selected by outsiders from the college who know nothing about how prison works.'

There was a battle when it was discovered that Myleen, an Australian from the college Human Resources Department, once known as 'Personnel', did want to put in her own person, a qualified teacher from Sri Lanka. Fran and Kantila, who were also on the selection panel, fought her off and got Comfort the job.

I was happy with my sessional work, although it only paid £20 an hour and had no security. Fran was deeply annoyed but was determined to use my talents. She didn't like the press, but she seemed to approve of journalism as an academic subject, so she suggested I should start teaching journalism to some of the lower groups, using an NUJ course called 'Pathways to Journalism'.

Like all the other prison courses, this is supposed to lead to the equivalent of a real qualification in the real world. Of course it doesn't, as the awarding bodies are not respected by outside academic institutions, and journalism is not and never will be an academic subject. But everything has to lead to a fancy-sounding qualification, even if there is no chance in reality of it meaning anything. At least it was a new way of presenting literacy to the men, and I hoped they would enjoy it.

'I 'ate journalism, Miss,' said Ronnie, a skinny white youth who put his head on his pasty arms and groaned when I told them the plan. 'The papers are shit. I never read 'em.'

The others agreed with him. None of them had ever bought a paper themselves apart from the *TV Times*, except for one Nigerian who said that years ago he thought he had once read *The Sun*.

Ignoring them, like a comedian dying at the start of his act, I pressed on, laying out a selection of magazines and papers, tabloids and broadsheets across two desks. Some of the papers, such as the free *Metro*, were banned, for obscure reasons set out by Mr Zippo when he was in one of his fulminations. They all started grabbing the sports and television pages. None of them even peeked at *The Sun*'s page three, in their usual way of eschewing sex – or it could have just been modesty as I was there.

'Now, who reads *The Times, The Sun, The Mail*?' I asked. 'What sort of people?' Surprisingly, this got them started. Although I had been warned not to sound like a social worker in the staffroom, in case of causing 'offence', the men loved discussing different groups in society, seeing it as a way of having a go at people they despised.

'*The Times*, that's all toffs innit, Miss?'

'What about *The Sun*?' Embarrassed silence. 'What sort of a paper is that?' On the whiteboard, I wrote 'xenophobic', which, surprisingly, they all found highly amusing. I also tried 'metrocentric', 'exclusive' and 'scoop'. But it was 'xenophobia' that they really liked, rolling it over in their mouths and laughing heartily, cherishing it as if it was the name of a new fantasy football club. Some of the white lads wanted it as a label for themselves, while the foreigners used it against Britain.

'You British hate outsiders. Your papers are full of lies about asylum-seekers,' sneered Pim. He had been born in South Africa but educated in Germany. He could have been Middle Eastern. Short and fat, with a large head and pock-marked skin, he had a grobian grin which he flashed when he was being very unpleasant.

We looked across a range of papers at the story of Madeleine McCann, who had recently been abducted. 'You British believe anything,' he went on nastily. 'You think this man is guilty or that man because you read it in the papers.'

The rest of them, apart from the white boys who were snoozing, agreed on how stupid the British and their news-papers were.

'There is no free speech in this country,' he jeered on. 'You can't say anything here. 'If I walk up to a policeman in London and say, "What is your problem, you dumb ass," he will take my name and all my details. If I did that in Germany, the policeman couldn't take any details from me, he wouldn't say anything.'

The whole class agreed, and we had to listen to a short talk about how great Germany is compared to the UK. I felt myself getting rather hot. A Polish lad was watching me, with a worried look, but said nothing. The Second World War has been over for a long time, but I felt that old subtext rising.

'People only come to this country to get the money,' Pim went on.

'And why did you come here?' the Pole asked, rallying a bit.

'I am innocent of everything,' he replied, suddenly in a rage, waving his short arms. 'They cannot get anything on me. I had no idea what was in the lining of that suitcase. What kind of an idiot tries to bring that much stuff in anyway?'

There was a meaningful silence, then he said that in future he was going to do a maths class instead.

When we got down to some journalism, the men were not sure what interviews were, and it was surprisingly hard to find any in the papers, apart from one in *The Telegraph* about the wife of a British diplomat who had found out that her husband was unfaithful. This was presented with a large soft-focus photo of the wronged wife on the front lawn of a palatial house accompanied by her red setter. The dog and wife had roughly the same hairstyle and looked mournful. Not a good advert for exciting, cutting-edge features, and the men gazed at it blankly.

I had my own experiences to fall back on and described some past interviews and the problems that can occur: Hollywood stars who would offer you an hour, which would slowly be whittled down throughout an anxious day to ten minutes – how all you can do then is hope to get a line, some little thing that they say which is of interest, and then back it up from cuttings.

I told them that celebs can often be just too difficult. I recalled how Bob Monkhouse had suddenly refused to see me because he decided that I 'didn't know enough about his life', although I'd spent a week in the cuttings library and had been fascinated by his radio interview with Dr Anthony Clare on BBC Radio 4.

There was the meeting with that bluff old American crooner Howard Keel who suddenly decided he wouldn't have his photo taken. A nasty dispute broke out between Keel and the snapper before he went stamping off to his vast tour bus. As he drove away, he gave us a wonderful shot, mightily giving us both the finger.

I told them what the editorial hand can do, how my sympathetic, perceptive interview with Arthur Scargill, which revealed a lot about his difficult childhood, was changed by the editor to make him sound like a dangerous lunatic and published under the banner headline: 'The Dinosaur Returns.'

I told them about the perils of sympathising too much. Arthur had complained to the Press Council. I wrote to him apologising, and he used my letter as evidence against me.

They sat quietly listening, and, encouraged, I even sketchily outlined a well-known French actor I slept with after interviewing in Paris. He gave me some extraordinarily pillow talk, revealing that he'd gotten married two days before and was about to go on his honeymoon. The men looked impressed, except an African named Pius, who walked out in disgust, saying I was 'loose'. It was the only story that got any real response, and then I realised that of course they didn't know the names of anyone I'd mentioned.

Group exercises also proved tricky. I tried to get them to interview each other in pairs but they only asked about the length of the other man's sentence and quickly started chatting about how they'd been abused by the legal system. They did throw up a few interesting stories: a Latvian youth came to the UK with his girlfriend, and they were both in prison for possessing false passports.

'There were many passports in the house. They covered the whole floor of one room when the police came,' he told me, always looking nervously just off to the side of my head. I wondered how his romance was going now they never saw each other.

'Prison bad for boy,' he said, 'but much more bad for girl.'

An Angolan told me he'd taken a degree in Philosophy at Lwanda University and was at London University doing a BA in Law and Politics until he ran over a pedestrian whilst driving without a licence or insurance.

'I am always such a careful driver,' he said mournfully. 'I was so surprised to be sent to prison.'

He was writing an extensive essay entitled 'World Economic Equality: Opportunities for All.' His handwriting was beautiful, but there was little meaning in the sentences. I suspected he was slightly deranged and wondered how London University had accepted him.

'I won't be going to Maths,' said the South African German at the end of the class, flashing his grin. 'I find this class very interesting.'

No amount of description or exercises can amount to the value of actually doing something yourself. Journalism is, above all, a craft, a practical skill. It can be done well even by people who cannot write well – what is needed is experience. I got the men to interview a friendly prison officer about his life, and they could interview visiting speakers, but these were rare events. Because we couldn't get out, mostly it had to be about embedded literacy and came down to a discussion about writing styles, how information is put over and the ideas behind this, which always veered dangerously close to conspiracy theory.

Another staff teaching job came up, and this time I filled in the form carefully, point by point, box by box. Again, it demanded things that I could hardly comprehend: 'The ability to teach up to national Skills for Life Level 2 including Key Skills Communications.'

I had to be 'responsible for prison-related administration' (never done any of that and hopefully never would). 'Liaise with Verifying Bodies where appropriate' – that sounded a bit elevated for an ordinary teacher, but I didn't mind liaising, as long as they didn't ask me anything very tricky. 'To recommend to the Literacy Coordinator on the purchasing of teaching and learning materials and to keep inventories of all equipment purchased' – I had already ordered books and CDs, laboriously writing out several forms and a letter to Kantila, but nothing had ever reached me through the internal mail. I was required to 'keep abreast of current developments within the field of Literacy and develop appropriate resources' (a good job they couldn't see my trusty old grammar book). The personal skills required included initiative, motivational, communication and management skills, the ability to work as part of a team, willingness to 'attend any required training' (more chicken legs and kiwi fruits) and, strangely, they also wanted 'good humour'.

This time I was called for an interview. The letter said it would last forty-five minutes and I would have to introduce or, as they put it, 'contextualise' my lesson then present an icebreaker followed by a fifteen-minute 'micro-teach' or mini-lesson.

'Whatever you do, keep it simple,' said Fran. 'You haven't got much time, and they are thick bastards.'

I decided to do my metaphor class again, as it had gone down so well previously.

For the icebreaker, I would bring in some trays of ice and get the panel to smash them. A metaphor, right? I thought I would do this first for dramatic effect – to make a great entry – before going into the contextualisation. Then I would get on with the lesson itself. It was the kind of thing you might do in writing: a lively intro followed by a brief explanation of what the story is.

I had a problem 'contextualising', as this had to be couched in specific educational terms. Fran rehearsed me, and I watched enviously as the right words just fell from her lips: 'As part of my teaching English writing for different purposes, at Literacy Level 2, we are looking at English in-depth whilst taking account of mixed ability, differentiation, different learning styles, etc., etc.'

I also had to find a freezer in the prison for the ice trays and get some way of breaking the ice without breaking rules as no hammers or sharp implements were allowed. In the end, I just settled for bringing in a cool bag and a sharp-edged wooden ruler.

A few days before the interview, the College rang to say they had lost my application form and would I mind filling it all in again? I very nearly dropped out at the thought of those columns and endless dates and lists of old exam results. Fortunately, just as I sat down to begin again, they rang to say the form had been found. That was a relief, but I felt desperately nervous – not in the slow nagging way a journalist feels before a big interview but in that panic that comes before a driving test or making a speech, or both combined.

'You'll be fine,' said Comfort. 'Once you get going, you will shine.'

'I have every confidence in you,' said Fran.

'You should be used to that type of thing at your age,' said my mother. Strange how that is never true.

Someone else advised me to breathe slowly up one nostril whilst closing the other. I knew that it was just a small interview for a small job (at least it had a very small salary) and that very little could go wrong.

I thought the panel would be the same as the one that appointed Comfort – Myleen, Kantila and Fran – but, as I sat waiting on the landing above the Officers' Mess, I saw Kantila stride past, smiling but not looking at me. I called out to her. 'Nothing to do with me,' she called back. 'I've just been told that I'm not on the selection panel. I'm out of it.' She shook her long ringlets in annoyance and walked on. That was a bit of a blow.

I was shown into a tiny room, which managed to seem airless even though the window was open. Myleen, Fran and Rod, Kantila's new deputy, were sitting at a narrow table. In front of them was a mobile whiteboard, lopsided on an uneven bit of floor, with a large crack across it.

I smiled at them. Fran looked down at her papers. Rod looked blank and nervous while Myleen looked positively stony, like someone on a parole board looking at a particularly unsavoury prisoner.

I wrote 'metaphor' on the wobbly whiteboard, which fell sideways. Rod shot up to stick it straight again. 'I struggled through fire and water to get here today,' I joked. Blank faces. 'Well, this place is a hive of industry!' Blank faces, Fran still looking down.

Moving hastily on, I got them to break the ice. Fran had a go, tentatively using the corner of the ruler, laughing nervously, but the others just stared at the tray as if I was offering them something unpleasant to eat. There was no participation and not a flicker of amusement.

I got into the 'contextualisation', which seemed to me to hold up the flow of the lesson. 'I have come here today to teach metaphor and extended metaphor,' I said enthusiastically. 'Do you think I can shed some light on this subject?' In my prison class, the men had shouted 'Yes', to this, and I had shouted back, 'Well, what do you think I am then, a light bulb?'

No response this time, and this audience looked as if they would like to throw non-metaphorical tomatoes. They seemed to be in some strange state of paralysis. I was getting hotter, but there was a terrible noise from an industrial lawn mower outside so I closed the window firmly, hoping also that this might show that I was 'controlling the teaching environment', as it said in the textbook.

I sat down facing them, and it was a very narrow table – in fact, we were almost nose to nose, which didn't feel quite right, as if this was a really unpleasant dream.

I began to lead them through the poem by Vernon Scannell, hoping someone would quickly volunteer to read and we could get on to a lively question-and-answer session. There was a lot of hesitancy before Myleen reluctantly read the poem in a strained strine.

I asked them to find the metaphor in the first four lines ('flame', 'fanged', 'tigers'), but before anyone could answer, to my surprise, the class was over.

It ended in what seemed like five minutes not fifteen, and they were on to the next job of asking me qualification questions. I was almost sure now that this was a dream and I'd wake up soon ready for the real interview. As it turned into them questioning me, it was unpleasantly real:

Myleen: Why do you want this job?

Me: Well, I really enjoy working in the prison. *(She frowns.)*

Rod: Can you give evidence of your skill at team-building?

Me: Well, no, I can't really, except that we all have to pull together you know, all hands to the pump, everyone helps everyone along. I ask other teachers for advice. *(He frowns.)*

Fran: How do your lessons in English and Art relate to the wider curriculum in subjects such as IT and Maths?

Me (Dumbfounded. I thought she was my friend so why is she asking me something like that?)

She tried to clarify the question. 'How do you think the Learning and Skills Curriculum assists learning?'

Myleen jumped at her. 'You are helping her. You are not allowed to do that.'

'She's right, you can't do that,' put in Rod, as if he was scared by the HR lady.

'I've no idea about curriculum really,' I said. 'I haven't come across it yet. I just work from lesson to lesson, trying to find topical, interesting themes and new ways of embedding literacy. But obviously all the things we teach in Literacy feed into other areas.'

Rod and HR frown. I can't see Fran's face as she is looking down again. A few minutes later, back in the Education

Department, Rod tells me that I haven't got the job.

'You told us what you were going to do rather than doing it,' he said, as if talking to a stupid child. Wait a minute, I thought, no I didn't! There was an icebreaker, which was self-explanatory, and the first part of a micro-teach, which was suddenly stopped.

'Don't worry,' he said, sounding jocular, 'I am crap at job interviews too. I applied for hundreds before I finally got this one.'

I looked at him in astonishment. What was he saying about himself and working in the prison?

'You didn't seem to know enough about team-building,' he went on, while the words 'utter pillock' formed in my mind.

'What exactly does that mean?' I asked him. No reply. I asked again, three times and still no answer.

'Look, I'm not going to argue about it,' he said crossly. 'You didn't seem to know much about the curriculum, and the National Curriculum wasn't referenced in your lesson plan.'

He'd got me there. He bunged two large spiral-bound folders at me about 'curriculum planning and management' in ESOL and IT. Did he seriously think I was going to sit and read them when I don't even teach ESOL or IT? I'd rather be stabbed in the eyes with my Jimmy Choos.

'Now, don't be difficult,' I heard him say as I swept out of the room.

'She just didn't want you,' said Fran, shedding real tears of frustration.

'She was against you from the start because we got our way over the candidate last time. Kantila was bumped off the panel, and they put Rod on. He was supposed to support your application, but I don't think he knew what he was doing. But she didn't like anything about you. She even hated the way you closed the window. She said you should have consulted more broadly before you did a thing like that.'

Apart from the window, I'd done other bad things too: 'You shouldn't have said you liked working in the prison,' said Fran. 'That was not a good answer. You should have given a detailed description of your work and why you think it has been successful.'

But the real disaster was starting with the icebreaker. Because I'd started with a metaphor, they couldn't have been more bewildered if I'd done the whole thing on ice. To be in modern education is to get everything in the right order. Dramatic effect or not, I was supposed to 'contextualise' first, and, because I didn't do that, they took my 'contextualisation' to be my lesson, hence Rod saying 'You explained what you were going to do rather than doing it.'

They had counted the contextualisation within the fifteen minutes of lesson, so that the lesson, when it came, was cut short. I felt I had let Fran down and that things had unravelled slightly. My enthusiasm for the place had taken a knock. But at least no outsider had got the job as the only other candidate had not shown up at all.

Fran and Gerald thought I might have a case to complain about the interview as the quarrel over the previous job application seemed to have carried over into mine and there had been so much confusion. Fran applied for me to have another micro-teach and I sent off an email to the formidable Glenda Gittings, the college administrator in charge of the education contract with the prison. I gave my account, laying the blame squarely on the shoulders of Myleen, who seemed to me to have been as anti-personnel as a landmine.

A few days later, Fran appeared looking dismayed again. Glenda was on holiday, and her emails had all been read by Myleen, who was reported to be 'very upset'. We agreed that I could probably wave any appeal goodbye.

8

Despite the débâcle of the job interview, Gerald organised an election for the post of union representative for Health and Safety and asked me to stand. I laughed at the idea: what had I got to do with the people who ban conkers and hanging baskets? I went along with the tabloid-newspaper joke: Q: What do safety managers and sperm have in common? A: Only one in two million ever does anything worthwhile.

I think they got the idea that I might be good at this job because of my grumbling about the lack of women's loos, declaring it to be unhygienic, unconstitutional, a breach of women's rights, etc., and the only other person standing for election was Fatima. 'She wants to become management,' said Fran bleakly. I won the ballot despite being just a sessional worker, the lowest of the low, not even a properly contracted employee, but it was probably a vote against my opponent rather than one for me.

A missive arrived in my pigeonhole claiming to be a 'response to the consultation document', which had apparently asked, 'Have we got the right legislation, guidance, encouragement?' – the answer to which question had apparently been no, because it was followed by another question: 'If not, which pillar or pillars need adjusting and how?' I'd had quite enough of metaphor but managed to grasp that this was something to do with a health and safety meeting for union officials, salmonella-free drum sticks provided.

I was soon huffing and puffing down the Gray's Inn Road to my first H&S meeting. Eventually, after cursing people who couldn't give any directions because they didn't speak a word of English, I found the right building: old and ornate on the outside, built at a time of civic pride, now truncated inside into a series of low, narrow rabbit hutches.

We pinned on our name badges and sat looking at each other: thirteen H&S practitioners. Tim, the man in charge for the day, stood by the whiteboard, smiling reassuringly, looking a bit East Berlin chic in little round specs and tight leather waistcoat. You could see he was unhappy about something.

'There has been no fire drill, and there should have been. We've never had one yet,' he said sadly. Perhaps it was that, but I think his unhappiness probably went deeper.

We introduced ourselves, table by table, thankfully without an icebreaker this time and it seemed that almost everyone in the room was an academic from a London university, mostly writing PhDs about stress. Apparently, stress at work (malingering as my mother's generation called it), now costs employers £5.8 million a year, which if nothing else proves that throwing sickies is a national craze.

'Stress is a notifiable disease,' said one of the men indignantly. I remembered seeing that term stamped inside filthy old library books, under the instruction to put the book down immediately if you were suffering from TB or cholera.

Like most of the other men, he looked very earnest, dressed in the regulation open-necked shirt, cheap-looking slacks, socks and sandals – the kind of dress worn by most educated men these days it seems, from vicars to television interviewers.

A lady tutor from Birkbeck wore elegant, slightly ethnic clothes from Liberty or Monsoon, while the other women looked more like the tutors I'd seen lately in my college: scrub-headed, tattooed, wearing boob-tubes and tight jeans.

Opposite me sat Susan, a large youngish woman from Belfast, dressed in a kind of pinafore, her greasy hair dragged into a topknot. She sat with her hands clasped before her, as if she was praying.

When I said I worked in a prison they loved it. I could see lights of approval go on. They couldn't have liked me more if I spent my holidays giving out care packages to orphans in African townships.

'Do you have to go there every day?' asked the pretty Birkbeck lady. She reminded me of the time I interviewed Julie Andrews and told her that I'd just come back from visiting friends in Poland. 'Were they very real?' she said in her suddenly intense Californian way.

No one asked me any specific questions about the working conditions inside or about the type of education we served, so I knew they weren't really interested. For liberal people, teaching in prison was just a nice idea.

Tim said we were there to try to work out a strategy for getting H&S recognised as one of the 'essential components of modern education'.

'We want H&S integrated into the whole system,' he said, 'central to institutional policy. We must aim to get several H&S officers into every institution in order to "buddy," to bring about real change.'

It all sounded a bit sinister, as if he was harking back to Communist cells. But there was little need for any secret strategy as the Zeitgeist was surely going his way. There has been a 50 per cent increase in the number of H&S representatives in schools and colleges in 2006, and they have their own website.

At 10.30 a.m. we got into the inevitable 'workshops', writing down all our successes and failures at bringing H&S into the workplace. An hour later, we stood up, one by one, and professed knowledge or described situations we had witnessed or dealt with, for better or worse.

All I had was our prison lavvy situation. I hadn't done much about that yet, and it was proving a draining experience. Other people had more dramatic stories to tell: a lab explosion at the University of East Anglia, resulting in a court order. A vicious argument in the staffroom at Birkbeck which led to a ripped skirt and an internal investigation.

One representative had discovered an unreported case of Legionnaire's Disease in Nottingham University, another had been tipped off about nitric-acid burns in a classroom incident. There had been irresponsible removal of radioactive waste in a lecturer's briefcase, and a schoolboy had been caught with plutonium in his garden shed.

The large, flapping pages from a flip chart were plastered across the far end of the room, like Chinese wall posters. Susan stood at the front and went though the points made on our table. She obviously knew every piece of safety legislation passed since 1848.

Half listening, I realised that I felt unwell, my body changing without my permission, getting its times wrong, turning into a strange, unreliable place, rebelling against what had been the natural order of my life, a simple mark in my diary made every twenty-eight days. I had to get to a chemist to grab some tampons. In the distance I could hear Susan's voice pouring out the key H&S words: 'share', 'networks', 'risk assessment', 'rights', 'clarification', 'confidentiality' (a word which H&S people love as it sounds so grown-up and grave) plus two much-used but meaningless imports from the USA, 'line manager' and 'leverage', as in, 'I had to go back and ask my line manager for more leverage to get another loo put in.'

Susan also liked 'presentism' – or perhaps she said 'presenteeism', an entirely new word to me – meaning 'not absent'. This was yet another new language, to be attached to the new language of FE.

Lunch was supposed to present itself at 12.30, but at 1.45 p.m. there was no sign of it. I saw other people looking around uneasily. Tim called again for us 'practitioners of H&S' to 'bring about change'. Then, before I could escape to the chemist or get stuck into the chicken legs, we were into another workshop, to discuss 'bullying and related stress in our sector'. Everyone looked very stressed, hungry and annoyed.

As had been hinted in my first college class, rather than eager pensioners, FE teachers face increasing hordes of what are known as 'second-chance students' who've failed or been excluded from school, and these charmers can assault teachers with impunity by email or with their fists. Several of the male teachers complained about violent students who cannot be excluded from FE classrooms.

Of course, I didn't have this problem in prison, with the baton-wielding mufti-men in charge. None of this applied to the Scrubs where, if the men misbehaved, they got excluded from Education, which meant a loss of money and the boredom of the cell. Or, in extreme cases, they got beaten up by the officers, the extreme deterrent which never fails to keep order – a situation unthinkable to these H&S people. The professional roughness that even I, as a journalist, had known during the stress of getting a paper out, was probably unknown to them. What they seemed to encounter in their idealised world of education was personal politicking and furtive expressions of jealousy.

We were finally freed for a break and trooped out past the Polish caterers who were sitting outside smoking. Over lunch, the talk was of exploding gas canisters and personal-accident claims. Susan was something of a hero because she had managed to combine compensation culture with political correctness when she had successfully sued the *Daily Mail* and won a big sum. She'd done this after the paper reported that in a speech she had accused accountants of being boring. 'Of course,' she told me, 'I am a bit of trouble-maker me, but I would never use a stereotype like that.'

Tim, our leader who hailed from Manchester, told me he had been in H&S since he was twenty. In those days the job had been entirely different. He had been a shop steward in the mining industry and his job then was about harsh working conditions, chemical hazards, pit-props, lung disease and fire escapes – real matters of life and death – now, he said, it's all about 'psychosocial injuries, mainly caused by mice'.

'Electronic abuse is quite as bad as getting punched in the face,' said one weedy man with a Ted Baker briefcase, who looked as if he'd probably cry if someone shouted at him.

I wondered about these people, who might once have been fighting to end the slave trade, widen the franchise and legalise trade unions, now getting in a twist about 'emails that cause outrage'. Is H&S a displacement activity, a reflex resulting from helplessness, because it seems that nothing can turn us back from the way we live now: the culture of downsizing, outsourcing, hot-desking, pension-shrinking and performance-related pay. Nothing can give Tim his real job back, or the time when his ideas were fed by a lively political culture.

We all have to adapt. I went home via Hammersmith Hospital, where a Japanese friend had just had a hysterectomy. She looked paler than usual but more beautiful, with her hair like wet black moss. Her room was full of flowers. Women stood round each other's beds smiling and making light chat. A young-looking woman from the Caribbean told us she had had eight children including one miscarriage. We stared at her, interested, sympathetic even but not really connecting to her story, as we were both childless single women.

'The decision about children has been made for me,' my friend said, insisting that she was not upset.

The next day, given courage by her, I visited the hospital again to get an appointment for a scan to find out what was going on inside my insides. Later, a young doctor with a handsome jaw said it was not the dreaded menopause, not yet, only fibroids. I was revolted. Other people get things like that, not me. It sounded as pathetic as piles. I told him rather accusingly that when I'd had an ovarian cyst removed in 1981 there was nothing extra in there then. 'That was then,' he said dismissively, unable to see the injustice of it.

As I walked back from the hospital, along the grimy Du Cane Road, past the prison, I saw my insides, or at least that void called a womb, as a fossilised forest full of stone stumps and branches – a cold, dark place where no one would ever live.

I was able to shove most of these dreary feelings aside, perhaps because of my maternal feeling for the men and my place in the prison, where I felt needed. It was in some ways a refuge for me as well as for some of the men.

I was also starting to have a sociable time. I often walked up to Notting Hill with Fran, stopping at one of her favourite health-food shops to buy a particular brand of tofu. She loved the area, even the names associated with it: Ladbroke, Elgin, Portobello, which she lovingly called 'The Bello', and although she and her partner could only afford to rent there, she refused to live anywhere else.

'I should have married a rich man,' she'd say, laughing bitterly, 'I had my chance.'

We'd walk along Talbot Road, admiring the early Victorian terraces bathed in yellow light, past villas with narrow Italianate windows or little Regency-style balconies. 'It's not fair that some people have so much,' she said, 'while others have nothing. I want to live here. Why can't I live here? It's so unfair.'

She sounded like people down the ages, one of the Parisian women gazing on Marie Antoinette's bedroom, or perhaps a hungry Muscovite breaking into the Winter Palace.

'I'd like to kill the kind of people who live here,' she'd say sometimes, her small brown face creased up with rage. 'They got all their wealth from slavery. They deserve to die.'

I was also stabbed with envy at the sight of pretty pink-washed houses and smart terraces with their newly trimmed spiralling shrubs in neat pewter tubs. Places that cost £3,250 in 1956, the year I was born, were now on sale for £2.9 million. To live in one of those . . . what kind of life would that be?

'You never had that kind of luck, so don't even think about it,' the houses answered back stonily.

Both of us knew that we would probably never own a house in London, where we had lived so long. As professional people we had been well paid. I had been very well off. It was an odd situation to be in, unknown to previous generations, and it gave a helpless if not hapless feeling. But most of our time was spent with men and boys who had never had luck of any kind all their lives from when they first opened their eyes to get a hazy view of Mum.

One day in Ladbroke Grove we saw Vere, standing in a shop doorway. He was wearing his usual smart leather jacket but he looked diminished. When I greeted him, he smiled but was shivering like a nervous whippet. I said, 'Let's have a coffee,' but Fran shushed me as it was against the rules to have contact with ex-cons.

We stood with him in the doorway for a while, smiling encouragingly, asking how things were going. He told us that while he was in the Scrubs his flat had been stripped of all its contents down to the last teaspoon. He had no bed, no curtains, no cutlery or plates. He now had been robbed by 'friends' who knew he was going to be away for some time.

According to Fran, this looting when men are incarcerated is quite usual, but Vere seemed shaken and depressed by it. I suggested he might go to a charity shop. He looked surprised as if he didn't know anything about them. Perhaps they are only used by middle-class people looking for bargains. Besides, he had no money left from the £40 that prisoners are given when they leave, and he had to wait at least ten days for any money from Social Security to come through. In prison, he'd told me he had the chance of a job with a drugs-counselling group, but now he seemed uncertain about it, cut adrift. Fran gave him some addresses and phone numbers, and we left him, no more contact allowed.

Not everyone was so friendly towards me. Wherever you work there is always one person who might be termed a fly in the ointment. Fatima was not happy about my spectacular win in the H&S election, and I seemed to have moved from 'big hugs' with her back to silence and watchfulness.

I saw that she hated anyone she thought was showing her disrespect, but they could do this so easily, by the raising of an eyebrow or even a friendly tone of voice which she would take as patronising.

'She hates anyone who doesn't look like her,' said Comfort. 'It's a kind of religion based on skin colour, and when it gets into people it destroys their minds.' She was saying, without saying it, that Fatima didn't like white people, or even people like Comfort, who weren't as black as she was.

One afternoon, as I was signing my name in the register at the end of classes, Fatima pushed in front of me, apparently not seeing me. Maggie Woo, a Chinese teacher, was standing beside me and got in her way.

'Manners, manners,' she shouted and shoved Maggie violently sideways. I could feel her fury and hatred for us, and I felt afraid of her. Maggie decided not to report it as she was too scared of making a fuss and she suspected that Kantila would always defend Fatima. Fortunately, I didn't have to see Fatima very often, but in a small department you can't help seeing people. One morning, rushing out of my classroom to the loo, before lessons started, I saw her standing on the other side of the locked gate. 'Excuse me, could you open the gate for me?' I called.

'Find someone else,' she replied, looking down her long straight nose at me.

'Thank you so much!' I called cheerily at her narrow back, knowing how easily she would hear mockery in my voice.

After six months in prison, I allowed myself a week off from it all and went to Venice, to write my first travel piece since I'd changed jobs. I didn't tell anyone at the prison, as, even if they liked me, they all had a lingering suspicion about the press. I allowed myself to be a journalist again for a short time, with luxurious free accommodation laid on. I stayed in Palazzo Mocenigo, where Byron once stayed, a small private mansion with a grand hallway under an inch of water. After my initial joy at being there, I felt acute disappointment: St Mark's Square seemed to have been taken over by American college kids talking about food and beer who shared it with Japanese tourists in identical sun visors and safari suits trooping past like a small unpleasant army. I struggled around in icy rain, battling through narrow streets clogged with umbrellas. The only afternoon that I felt I had seen anything authentic was when I took the wrong waterbus and ended up on an hour's journey around the boondocks looking at cranes and scrapyards. A refreshing change from being in a museum – I mean both Venice and the Scrubs. Because of the weather, no one sat out in the cafés, so it was hard to chat to anyone. My only conversation seemed to be with swindling waiters and the proliferating living statues and herms who stood about with their white paint flaking and running in the wet.

I spent my last evening in Harry's Bar, where Hemingway once concocted his frozen martini, relishing its gelatinous texture. Tourists swarm there now for the chance to down the bar's more famous Bellini. Claudio Ponzio, the barman, told me that he was obliged to serve 700 of them a week in the season.

Jane, the lonely spinster played by Katherine Hepburn in the film *Summer Madness,* drowned her sorrows there and fell in the canal nearby. George Eliot's second husband threw himself into the Grand Canal on their honeymoon. By the jaded look on his face I thought Signor Ponzio might go the same way. Venice is not called the drowning city for nothing.

On my way back in the dark to my cavernous, silent *palazzio*, I stopped in a long, narrow street struck by the beauty of a voice coming from a young man standing on a box singing, 'Remember Me', Dido's lament by Purcell. This is perhaps the saddest thing ever written, so sad that once on *Desert Island Discs* the singer Elvis Costello said it should only be sung about once every ten years. Listening to its tormented strains I put my head against a cold shop window and wept.

While I was doing this, a large woman, with an accent suggesting New Jersey, came and stood right next to me, peering into the shop.

'Can you see the price of those duvets? How much would it be to ship them and those sheets back home?' She was speaking to a man standing somewhere in the shadows.

She didn't seem to notice the crying or the singing going on. Perhaps like many Americans she just thought that all people abroad were mad and didn't give it any thought.

It was a relief to return to what I increasingly felt was the cosy warmth of the prison where no one is ever alone for long. But almost as soon as I returned I heard on the prison grapevine that Terry, the boy with the frail legs, had committed suicide. Whatever loneliness I felt, his had been far worse.

'Prison is a howling pit of need,' said Fran. 'Don't get sucked in.'

For several weeks after, I thought about becoming a psychotherapist in the belated hope of saving boys like Terry. I applied for a course and got accepted, but it was horribly expensive, and the prison wouldn't fund it.

'It's not relevant to what we do here,' said Kantila, which was certainly true, and no one was any more interested in therapy than in a new bog. I felt uneasily that I shouldn't have asked her. We never had proper conversations, which was disappointing and a bad sign.

Then witty and clever Hardip disappeared right in the middle of an Advanced English class with no time to finish the sentence he was writing, to collect up his things or to say goodbye. Everyone felt shocked and undermined. Education yet again subverted by Security – in this case by a clerical error. He was brought back that night as the prison receiving him knew nothing about his arrival.

Not long after that, I arrived back at my flat to find it flooded after very heavy rain. A tide of sewage water had burst upwards from blocked and clogged drains and had swept straight through. I stood there for a long while gazing down at the cold, soggy mess. It was like being in Venice again, but without any of the delights of decadent decay. There must have been about a foot of dirty water before it subsided, now rapidly being absorbed by skirting boards and plaster, carpets, rugs, books, papers, slippers. My cat Brenda had remained calmly on top of the bed but wouldn't climb down and put her paws anywhere near the warping floorboards. My winter duvet was soaked, so I pulled out some thin ones and threw them on in layers without their covers. They lay there like giant mille-feuille.

The next day, I realised that the whole street, including the local garage, had been flooded. Our pavements, usually strewn with torn black bags, were piled with carpets and rugs sopping with sewer water. Soon after, most of Gloucestershire and thousands of other homes went the same way.

My flat now smelled a lot like prison. I couldn't get away from the odour of mould and rot. This seemed to be a harbinger of bad tidings, as at work the mood in our peaceful if rigid little town called the Scrubs clenched a little.

A popular black teacher was reprimanded for playing the drums and dancing in his 'Life Skills' evening class, although he'd been doing it for a long time and his classes were full. Another was cautioned for bringing in sweets, and there was worse trouble because a Lemsip had been found in a cell and the scared prisoner had named the teacher who had given it to him. Prisoners would rarely 'shop' each other, but their strict code of *omertà,* did not extend to the staff, who had to look out for themselves.

'Could be an audit coming,' said Gerald. 'That's when Security have to be seen doing something.' Or it could just have been a Security move on Education, which sometimes happened, as they regarded the whole department as a security weak spot.

In the staffroom something unpleasant always seemed to be simmering. Marjorie was criticised by Kantila for 'scaring people'. To my mind she wasn't half as scary as Fatima. She was seen crying by one of the lockers and set about writing a letter of complaint to the College. I was sorry for Marjorie as I liked her now – even her hats, which made her look like a tawny Thora Hird. She had her own individual agenda, always fighting for something better in Education. She determinedly ignored Fran's dictum never to expect much in prison.

'At meetings I used to pipe up all the time asking if we could have drama and poetry workshops,' she told me in her clear Yorkshire tones. 'I have said we should be much more creative, but nothing ever come of it.'

I suggested she should go into politics if she really wanted to change anything. Her eyes lit up as she saw herself on a rostrum putting everything to rights with some common sense. I could see that she just needed a little encouragement but she never received any from the Management, who saw her as a nuisance and threatened to cut her hours.

Cutting a teacher's hours was Kantila's great sanction. It was done with no warning, and there was no redress. Marjorie greatly resented being talked down to by girls like Jailah, as we all did. It signalled a fundamental lack of respect for the teachers, and this came through in many ways. We were never consulted and were afflicted by constant puzzling changes directed from the world outside by the college Education Department.

My fast-track English class suddenly became 'Media Studies'. My afternoon English Level 2 was transformed into 'Communication'. Another ordinary English class became 'Citizenship', while everything else was lumped under 'Skills for Life'. There was never any explanation from Kantila, who seemed to take orders from the College grudgingly.

Fran had an elevated position as she had been there a long time and Kantila seemed to rely on her. But she had problems as well. Just after I returned from my holiday, she told me that she had met Loella on one of her lightning inspections of the Education Department. Suddenly Loella had turned on her and had started screaming abuse. As Fran walked away, she had heard a cry of 'Don't you turn your fucking back on me. I am reporting you.'

'If she plays the race card with me, she won't get far,' said Fran, sounding relaxed but determined. She could be reasonably sure that Kantila would be her ally in this one, against her own great enemy.

But that ominous card could be played many ways. Fran was dismayed when she got a call from the Prison Diversity Officer to tell her he was making moves to close down the prison magazine 'for racism'. A prison officer who was monitoring racism on the wings also got involved and said she was in 'a very serious situation'.

She had published a poem in *Free Time* called 'Hell and Back', written by a middle-aged black inmate about his life in England. Using a simple, elegant structure, with dates down the left-hand side of the page, he had carefully traced the change in social position and the varying levels of attention focused on black people in the UK from the time of his arrival in 1955.

> *It was hard to be black*
> *I was a bastard, told to find a banana boat and go*
>   *back.[. . .]*
> *2006.*
> *Prisons are full, multiracial melting pot;*
> *Hip Hop and Rap have made way for Grime*
> *which is just another sign of the time.[. . .]*

In the stanza marked '2000', he had written:

> *Nigger please Yo was up – don't push me*
> *'cause I'm close to the edge*
> *heroin, coke, crack and AIDS are on the attack*
> *race, colour, creed, step back.*

The Diversity Officer was on the phone as soon as the poem appeared, furious, calling it 'highly offensive', and launched 'a full enquiry'.

I thought it was possibly the best poem I had seen from a prisoner as it was so mature, well structured and gently ironic. Diversity officers don't 'do' irony, and Fran faced a battery of rage from those employed to be enraged.

She tried to defend the poem and herself but was told flatly not to allow anything 'like that' again. The author of the poem had been released before it appeared in the magazine so he missed all the hoo-ha and probably never knew what trouble his poem had caused, and, worse, he probably never knew how good it was. Presumably if he had still been inside he would have been ticked off well and told not to write like that again.

'Sometimes I feel like giving up,' Fran admitted.

Another job for Literacy Tutor came up in *The Guardian*, but I decided not to apply for it as I couldn't face going through that whole stressful rigmarole again. I wanted to teach, I was even told I was quite good at it, but I could not face the strangely oppressive prospect of *being* a teacher.

9

The art room, always popular with the men for their nefarious reasons, was now my place of refuge, full of interesting new faces. These included Mr Foch and Deano Banks, two frisky mixed-race boys of spectacular good looks. We also got Andrew Smith, only twenty-two, usually just known as Smith or Smithy as he was so grumpy. He was quite good at technical drawing, anything fiddly and intricate. He liked to sit hunched over complicated drawings of machinery and tricksy diagrams by George Escher. A former motorcycle courier, he was inside for obsessive speeding on his small bike which might have been something like a moped. His big claim to fame was being chased on it by five police cars up the M1 and refusing to stop.

People quickly learned never to get him onto the subject of bikes as it released an obsessive and often unintelligible outpouring. He discovered that he liked carving. Using a school compass, which had to be booked out of the locked 'shadow cupboard' in the office, he began to produce objects cut out of cheap bars of soap. He began to take requests, and most of the men asked him to carve out the names of loved ones within a small frame. His first one said: 'BALRAJ 4 NOVJOT FOREVER'. He began to churn out these small pieces in exchange for tobacco.

Mr Foch was eager to learn anything new, but his paintings were disturbingly dark: killer faces with iron, tearing teeth and bleeding knives. A lot of people commented on the disparity between the lively lad and his gloomy blood-drenched work. It was difficult to make him out. He said he wanted to be an architect and had applied to various colleges. He said he had been offered interviews but couldn't go to any because of being inside. Many of the prisoners were ambitious and had such dreams, but when they talked about their life outside the Scrubs, it sounded unlikely that they would ever be able to study.

'All my birds have been mad, Miss. I don't know why I pick girls like that,' he would say, sounding genuinely perplexed. 'The last one was crazy, she smashed our place up. I was worried about leaving her with the baby. I don't know why it turns out like that.'

Like the others, he wanted his partners to be good, competent mothers. I wondered if any of his girlfriends had been heroin addicts like him. He seemed shocked at the idea. 'Never,' he said. 'Wouldn't touch it, Miss.' But he admitted that he had sold heroin to girls.

'She was crawling about on her knees beggin' me for it, Miss,' he said. 'Beggin' me. Just begging.' He was awed by the level of the girl's desperation, but there was no remorse or empathy from him. Like many of the boys, he was from the modern equivalent of Gin Lane, where there is no pity and no work done, except by the porn broker or the drug dealer.

Deano, twenty-three, who had an Iraqi mother, was robust and handsome. Inside for possessing handguns, he loved guns and talked about them with a kind of gushing affection and some authority. He was already the father of four children by what he proudly called his 'baby-mothers'. He showed me a photograph of a baby who looked just like him, a miniature streetfighter with the same flat nose and bull neck. 'I never see him anymore, she won't bring him in,' he said sadly.

He was quite a gifted painter, picking up new techniques easily, despite the lack of books and materials. He would try different methods of painting, putting together striking images from black culture, Egypt and Mexico.

We now had a wide range of men studying art, of all ages and abilities. Mr Portman, a Jamaican, was forty but looked much older. He had a rather long, very black, lugubrious, craggy face but he was dignified too. He liked me to paint him but he noticed that in my paintings he always looked very 'lost'.

'You look like a slave,' I said, feeling rather uncomfortable about it. He laughed and agreed. Somehow the pictorial image of the American negro slave, which we both shared, kept coming through. He looked like that image, or it looked like him. One day he said, 'Oh great. You got it. That's the real nigger.' That taboo word again. Whatever its connotations, Mr Portman reclaimed it with satisfaction.

He was very good-humoured. When a younger man took one of his brushes, there could have been a nasty fight, but after some shouting he let it go.

We also had Ivan, from Liverpool, a little, middle-aged man who had deliberately caused half a million pounds worth of damage in Tate Britain when he had set about a painting by Willem de Kooning with pink and blue pastels.

'I thought it needed brightening up,' he said. 'I think I was having a breakdown. The gallery assistants grabbed me, dragged me out and shoved me into a little room. I thought, now for it, they are going to give me a right pasting, but instead they all took photos of me.'

He seemed to be sketching all the time, mostly using biro, catching men going through their day: sitting in their cramped cells, cooking, standing, sitting, playing dominoes, lining up for food, led off to the block and stripped naked. His whole day, if not his whole life, seemed to revolve around art, not in a morbid way like Rupert – he wasn't analysing or obsessing, just recording brilliantly.

As these new men were clamouring for extra work and John was finding new men on the wings, I started an evening class from 6 p.m. until 8 p.m. We were only allowed to do it one night a week.

Alone in the art room after most of the staff had gone home I discovered the eerie sounds of prison at night. The Education Department is silent and too far from the wings to hear any noise from there, so all you get is the wind howling through the building and everything seems to rattle and moan. There was also a rasping, cracking sound from beyond the barred windows as crows made a nocturnal skirmish in the gutters, a magpie making a sound like a child's rattle; a softer noise might be the twittering of birds in the eaves or distant keys jangling.

My first evening session was cancelled as there had been a suicide attempt in the afternoon, the second that week. A prisoner threw himself down from the fourth floor and was injured despite the protective netting strung below the landings. As he had been taken to hospital, the officers were short-staffed. They were always at least three men down on every shift so that if anything extra came up Education shut down.

It was difficult to know what my night-school men were going to do as there were so few objects to draw and I had no life model. I didn't know if it would follow the usual art-room pattern of men just sitting in groups doing their own thing or if they would for once let me have a go at teaching them. In the hope that we might get a group thing going, I piled up some large bones, skulls of cows and the model of a human skull and just hoped they would be interested.

I shifted the heavy easels from round the edges of the room, out of private corners, into a single group. I had a rather frantic hunt for free drawing boards as many of them were covered in bed sheets and used for painting. I had remembered to get in a supply of paper earlier as the art cupboard was locked after 4.30 p.m. I taped up the sugar paper to the boards, and, by 6 p.m., everything was ready. I even ventured near the radio, once the men's exclusive pre-serve, and found something called 'Smooth Radio', which sounded OK to me.

I still didn't know if any men would come. Half an hour late, they began trudging up, wing by wing. I had not seen many of them before and some were completely new to art. I set them up around the ossiary still life on the table. They always seemed puzzled by the charcoal, and I tried to get them to relax and explore its qualities. I quickly realised that they were more likely to do this than the men in my day class because they were really interested and had made a big effort to be there, shaking off the torpor of the cells. In fact the whole atmosphere was lighter as doing something out of the cells at night was a bit of a lark.

Errol, in a beautiful white cricket sweater, said he had never drawn from objects before, but he showed a real feel for it and immediately understood scale and measurement, things I'd rarely got through to anyone in the regular art class.

Ivan the Scouser brought along more of his vibrant drawings. They were so good that I felt rather envious. I wondered, as I always did with such men, why they weren't in art school proper or pursuing a creative career.

A very polite and handsome young South African arrived, so gracious that he reminded me of an Eton schoolboy. He was with an equally civil lad from Singapore: both in for drug smuggling and neither had ever been in trouble before. I suspected they were of a scientific bent as they struggled with the drawing as if it were a complex foreign language.

Isaac had been released before he could come to the evening class, and Bill, despite his own foetid locks, had gone off to do a prolonged barbering course. After a life-time in prison due to his drug abuse, this was possibly his last chance to find a useful trade. I was glad to hear he was moving on but sad that he had left without saying good-bye to me. Perhaps he thought it wouldn't matter to me. I missed them both and realised that this was a problem of working in prison, where people never felt valued and would disappear without a word.

As the men trooped away at 8 p.m. to be searched in the corridor, I felt the evening class had been a real success. Not only had more men been given access to art, but it had also been a very civilised, convivial atmosphere, with the students really concentrating for once, as a group.

Evening classes also brought along a lot of unfamiliar prison officers. For a few weeks we had an elderly black lady who was very amused and pleased by what we were doing. She chatted encouragingly and seemed almost angelically sweet, but she was replaced by a hostile young white man with a weasily face, who didn't like us at all. He wouldn't come into the room but stuck his sharp nose round the door at unexpected times to yell, 'Yer time's up. That's it, class over.' I heard that there was only one prison officer in the Scrubs who was a graduate, and it certainly wasn't him.

Officers could end the classes at will, after ten minutes or half an hour, or they might give you the full time – you never knew. Sometimes they just didn't bring the men up because they were too tired, too lazy or too pissed off. Extra classes were considered a drag and a bit eccentric, as if we were carrying this 'education for prisoners' caper a bit too far.

'The culture of prison is still against us,' said Glenda Gittings when I asked her about evening classes. 'Most officers are as institutionalised as the men, and everything has to be run according to them, on straight lines. I've heard them say, "What do the prisoners need education for?" They don't have educational skills themselves, so they just can't see the need. With them, it's all, "What's this for, what are you doing that for?"'

My quest was to find a life model. This was unknown territory in prison. The model couldn't be nude, as that would have caused too much hilarity, and I didn't know how the men would react to the idea of posing. It might have been seen as somehow effeminate – and so out of the question.

I asked AJ, a handsome young man with heavy dreadlocks who was in one of my English classes. (In fact, he was in almost every one of my classes as he followed me around.) He agreed to come along and was willing to take off his top clothes, shoes and socks and drape himself in an old sheet, showing part of his collarbone and one smooth, muscular shoulder. The men fell about laughing at this suggestion of real art-room nudity. AJ's small eyes crinkled up, and he whistled and hissed slightly through his metal-tipped front teeth to show his amusement. He perched on a high stool and arranged his locks in a way that made them look rather like a crown of thorns. Suddenly we had a black Christ sitting there, and his shadow on the wall behind made a dark shape worthy of a medieval shroud.

It was rather a disturbing image and very challenging to draw, but everyone got going on it, and soon there was a mood of intense concentration.

Through July and August I had enough men coming up to keep the class going, and everyone was working from the model for the first time. AJ was as reliable as he could be – he never got sent to the block or felt too lazy to turn up. I was warned by Kantila not to ask him to pose in any unusual way – there was to be no lying down as the officers on duty would regard that with great suspicion and report it to Security. He was happy to sit on his hard stool without moving for almost two hours. He refused a break, as if modelling was a macho challenge.

One evening when he didn't appear I saw a man strolling past and asked him to come in and sit for us. Without a word, he came in and sat on the stool. He was very black and box-shaped. I found out later that he was known as 'Shorty'. He took up the pose and seemed to be in some kind of trance, not sure why he was sitting motionless on a stool for two hours, surrounded by strange staring people.

It turned out that he had been on his way to a Narcotics Anonymous meeting when I stopped him. He came back later to see the drawings we had made and seemed pleased but still did not speak. He became a regular model when AJ couldn't come but remained silent for weeks. Sometimes before the evening class he'd come in and sit with me quietly. He became an enjoyable if mysterious presence.

Another night when AJ didn't come I went down the corridor and found the Narcotics Anonymous group in full swing (or loll might be a better word). 'Can anyone please come and model?' I implored. I saw Shorty and looked at him hopefully, but he slowly shook his head as if to say, 'I am obliged to stay here tonight.' A lot of tattooed syringe-stabbed arms shot up. The teacher looked very puzzled but let one man go with me.

Tony Ten Boom, known as 'the Big Dutch', also started coming up in the evening. When he'd switched the radio over and no one had challenged him, I had registered him right away as someone who could help to change the culture in the art room. He smiled at me in a slightly melancholy way.

'Is that Debussy?' I said. 'Yes, it is,' he answered, winking at his neighbour to indicate that he didn't really know but was keeping the lady happy. When he hit on a classical station, sometimes the men would respond either with horror and distress or with ridicule. We had to turn off *The Rite of Spring* before it provoked a second riot. They quickly rejected one of the Interludes from Brittain's *Peter Grimes,* but later when I told young Mr Foch the story of Grimes he was interested.

'I do like to hear about new things like that, Miss,' he said. 'I would like to go to an opera one day, I really would.'

I wanted to take the men to art galleries and to the theatre, experiences that most of them had never had – never would have – but it was, of course, a hopeless fantasy.

If there was too much protest about classical music, Tony would find something fairly melodic, perhaps a bit of Abba, which everyone could hum, or sometimes the sinuous voice of Amy Winehouse would wind and twist out towards us.

With the gentle music, we also now had easy communal talk around the big art table. Apart from mulling over the latest conspiracy theory (Deano was convinced that the war in Iraq was a move by Israel to destroy Islam), they usually talked about television they had seen the night before.

These failed bosses and gang leaders from the streets loved gangster films. They would sit up till the early hours instead of getting their beauty sleep watching *Scarface, Prizzi's Honour* and *Goodfellas*, able to quote every line. For some of them, the great mob bosses of US history represented the highest possible success of the immigrant.

Tony hated such things. 'I can't stand films about crime and drug dealers,' he said with contempt and self-loathing.

Television is very important to prisoners, and as they don't get out much its impact is magnified. Television producers are probably not even aware of this audience. When the soft-porn historical series *Rome* was on, I felt a palpable shift in the sexual temperature of the place. It made the men unruly. I heard them talking about scenes they'd seen the night before; they wanted me to discuss it with them, but I felt wary about being drawn in. It had made them more desperate, altering the fragile balance of the place.

After the film *The Passion of the Christ* was on, it caused intense discussion. Some men were quite upset, trying to explain it away as if all the cruelty had been exaggerated. Peter told me that it had increased his Christian faith.

Sometimes at the table they'd talk about women, but only in general, nothing specific about the ones they knew. They guarded that side of their lives carefully because it was precious and because they were so full of uncertainty about what was going on beyond the prison walls. I never came across anyone with a secure loving home to return to. Inside, women were the dream of ecstasy and the cause of acute anxiety.

During these discussions, Tony usually retreated to a corner where he illustrated blue international letter paper with coloured ink. The first thing I saw him do was to repeat a strange motif of a prisoner standing between two

Prussian-looking policemen. It looked like something from a woodcut. He told me he'd created the image when he was arrested. A few days later, I realised that it resembled a German, or perhaps Swiss, woodcut of about 1903.

'That's true,' he said when I mentioned it. 'It is from 1903. How did you know that?' He was a clever flatterer. I could see that he intended to work on all my weak points.

'If you copy other people's images, your work will be of *no artistic* value,' I said. He scowled at me like a scolded child. I asked him to try drawing something from life, but he sulkily refused. 'I am not feeling too good,' he said. 'I've just heard that my mother has cancer. She is dying and won't live much longer.'

'You haven't heard any such thing,' I said, rather astonished at myself. 'She's fine. There is nothing wrong with her at all.'

He looks abashed, but I ploughed on: 'How old is she?'

'Sixty,' he said looking sheepish.

'Then you've got at least twenty years to go with her,' I said, hardly recognising myself.

'Well,' he said, with resignation. 'I never see her as she hasn't spoken to me for ten years.'

He showed me a photo of his mother and sister, very good-looking, healthy blonde women, laughing together in a smart-looking kitchen. I wondered what he could have done to make his mother withdraw from him so completely. There must have been some final straw. I had been adopted, had met my natural mother a few times but had not seen her for fifteen years. Tony and I had both had been dumped by our mothers, both had a mother-shaped space inside, but this wasn't the same. He must have been a beautiful child, and his own mother had surely cared for him once, until something had gone terribly wrong.

He started drawing on the blue airmail letters: strange tower blocks with blank windows towering over streets with flowerbeds, sometimes colourful pictures of his cell with a ladder bursting through a hole in the roof. He said he was sending an ink painting of some white flowers to his grandmother. I wasn't sure that I believed this, although he was the kind of man who might remain a grandmother's darling. Perhaps she was the only person left who still trusted him. His other letter, he said, was going to his son Trixie, for his twenty-first birthday.

'I bought him 1,000 ecstasy tablets for his twentieth birthday,' he said defiantly.

One of the other prisoners explained to me that this was so his son could sell them in clubs and become a small-time dealer like his dad. Hearing this, I saw Tony more clearly: part of an alternative lifestyle that sprouted in Amsterdam about forty years ago, perhaps a bit of a local character, making small deals on street corners, picking round flea markets hoping to find some valuable article that had somehow been overlooked, hoping for some kind of find that would change everything but always losing in the end.

He showed me a photo of Trixie, a smiling mixed-race boy, whom I thought looked wise and sad about the eyes. He asked me to help him copy a photograph of a New York jazz club to send to his son. He obviously adored black culture, the American variety, seen through screen images of Louis Armstrong and Gregory Hines in the Cotton Club.

'I suppose you are going home now, to have clever conversations with your friends about artistic values?' he said petulantly as we were packing up. Someone laughed at his goading remark, the mood lightened and suddenly there was a joke between us. 'You rise to the bait, and you fight back,' he said. 'That is very nice in a woman.'

Another time he said, 'Why are you so lippy?' and made a motion with his hand like a bird's beak opening and closing. 'Sexist bastard,' I thought but not as annoyed as I normally would be. Was it because his shoulders under the green nylon Barbour he wore for his morning gardening shift looked so extremely attractive that my beak snapped shut?

'You are obsessed by the Second World War,' he said to me one day, not critically but observationally. I couldn't remember talking about it with him, but ideas flowed between us, and he responded to me with a drug dealer's fine intuition. Perhaps he was the sort who can get pensioners to carry cocaine across continents. But he was right and I knew he was referring to the *Endlösung*.

I remember the moment when I found out about the Final Solution. I was eleven and I had been reading a book for children called *This Is Your Century*, by Geoffrey Trease, published in 1965, which had an ominous black pendulum on the front cover.

Mr Trease's book was presumably written to make children think, but in my case it caused not so much a 'thought shower' as an electrical storm. It blitzed my brain. I had no one to talk to about it. My parents were not interested. They'd seen the newsreels from Belsen and believed that the Nuremburg Trials had settled that matter, but their evasiveness and vagueness turned it into some kind of secret that I wanted to crack. Much later, I realised that my identification was also about loss. The camps were the place where families and whole tribes were wilfully destroyed. They were about the separation of families and detachment of mothers from children.

I also relished the heroism and strong individual identity thrown up by the crisis of the war; Tony and I talked about

Hannie Schaft, a Dutch girl executed three weeks before the end of the war and buried in sand dunes, along with nearly 500 other resistance fighters. I had looked for information about her in the Resistance Museum in Amsterdam, which is right opposite the zoo where Tony told me he had once worked cleaning windows. He'd never been in the museum, or in any museum that I knew of, but he said her name as if he was thumping his heart.

Tony had a good brain. If I asked him to calculate something he could do it in a flash, something unusual in English people. I got the hazy impression that something had gone wrong for him in primary school.

'The teachers were hitting me. My parents were upset; they would ask, "Why are you hitting my child?",' he told me, still indignant about it. Like many prisoners, he had failed in some way early on, and the humiliation had remained and had gone on damaging him. Despite that, he had become very bookish. He gave me a book called *Blue Mondays*, by his favourite author, Arnon Grunberg, a Dutch Jew who lives mainly in New York. Set in Amsterdam, where most of the Jews were swept away like leaves, the Holocaust acts in the text like a homoeopathic remedy, not really there at all except in the mind of the user. This projection shapes the whole thing, creating a strange morbid, necrotic atmosphere. The young Jewish protagonist, happily saved by being born at the right time in history, responds to the past with extreme nihilism, something that connected to Tony. He had somehow downloaded a list of Grunberg's novels, despite the fact that prisoners had no official access to the Internet.

'Have you seen his cell?' Deano asked me, with a disapproving smirk. 'It's crammed with stuff. You can hardly get in the door.' Apparently Tony's Aladdin's cave was stuffed with missing property from the art-room cupboard.

'I can get whatever I want,' Tony told me. 'It's no trouble, this place is soft.'

Mr Nusrat told me he had seen him at weekends, on a cleaning shift, making phone calls in the staff office. I wondered why he hadn't stopped him.

Tony obviously thrived on making deals and charming people. Sometimes, Groot the staffroom helper, another Amsterdam drugs dealer, would slide in, and they would chat in Dutch, sounding as if they were having a suppressed coughing fit.

However much I shuddered at his wheeler-dealer ways, we shared jokes and books and it started to feel almost as if we were in college, getting to know each other, inviting one another back for coffee, except, of course, there is no coffee and no inviting. We sat in the library, where Donna the Librarian claimed to have 'eyes in the back of her head'. We grabbed the nastiest tabloids and consulted them seriously for horoscopes. I hadn't done that since I was a student – in fact, since I was a virgin. He pronounced his star sign strangely, with a guttural sound unusual to an English ear: 'A-rees'. One day it said, 'A new relationship is bringing unexpected sunshine into your life.' We both looked down quickly.

10

I visited the library as often as I could because Tony practically lived there. I'd settle the men down, fetch papers, give Mr Bando some help to find African novels he hadn't read, then sit down next to Tony, rustling up against his green nylon Barbour.

'Aren't you supposed to be in art this afternoon?' I whispered one day.

'It's one of the Simons,' he muttered, speaking into his chest. 'I won't go if you're not there.'

We kept quiet most of the time, pretending we were not together, just absorbed in reading. To be so quiet was to be rather conspicuous because the prison library was a noisy place. Donna, small, bustling and good-natured, was usually either eating an all-day breakfast or on the phone talking in a high, penetrating voice about her next holiday or her last night out.

Some of the Africans trying to read would tut-tut, wishing she'd keep it down. Other men just took the chance to chatter, shout and laugh in their normal voices. In my first week I asked her if we could quieten it down.

'You can't expect a library to be quiet,' she said, spitting toast crumbs. 'You are way behind the times. There are no libraries like that now. Libraries are about drawing people in, not making people feel excluded.'

I discovered she'd once had a rather loud set-to with Marjorie about this issue, which had resulted in a letter from Marjorie to the College and Donna banning her from the place. I didn't want that to happen, so while loud voices burbled above us, mostly in Polish and Yoruba, Tony Ten Boom and I huddled low over the papers, unnoticed – we hoped.

Occasionally, men from my class would drift over to me whining, 'I wanna go back up now, Miss. Can we go up now Miss?' I'd look up at them witheringly as if they had the attention span of a gnat.

'Go and find yourself a book and sit down and read it quietly,' I'd snap, in the time-honoured teacherly fashion.

At the call for free flow, I had to go ahead of my men up the narrow, dark stairs to wait for the officer to unlock the gate at the top. Tony remained down below, standing in line, out of sight, which was frustrating.

Once a week I could get extra time with him at my evening class.

'In prison, everyone is in love with someone.' That was one of the first things Comfort told me when I arrived the previous September. Fran agreed. 'There is sometimes a spark with even the youngest men,' she said. 'There are a lot of romances going on all the time.' But she was too busy running things to be bothered by silly things like that.

Comfort's uncomfortable words played in my head like a Greek chorus. She didn't mean 'in love' in a carnal way – it is more about crushes. Prison love is a mirage – quite insubstantial – but I could easily see why it happened. After all, attraction to another gives a feeling of being strangely nourished, and it can take the edge off everything throughout the day and the night. Although I could walk out through the gates at 5 p.m. every evening, I could sympathise with the men's yearning. In the early hours, faces from my past often loomed up at me, charged with bad memories or with accusing me of failure, but when I was in love they all vanished like a lurid waking dream.

I often found the life of a single woman in London very raw, but the closed world of prison can provide a soothing, safe environment for a woman.

'You have my full permission to talk to my friend here for as long as you like but I am chatting up your mate.' That came from a youngish man with a grinning face, hair *en brosse,* in Groucho's bar. He fancied my friend who is ten years younger than me, and I was getting in his way. He let me know it in his ringing Romford tones. Such incidents are not unusual out on the town.

'OK, lose the oik,' I said to my friend, 'we're going.'

I liked the surprise on his silly face as I said it, but, still clinging to my fourteen-year-old's notion that sexual recognition is a badge of honour, I felt as if I had been stabbed by him and more afraid of that increasingly raddled face of mine staring back from the Groucho Club's long bar-room mirror.

Working in the Scrubs was in some ways like taking a foreign holiday in that once you cross the Channel you find that there are a lot of men who really like women. Suddenly I was as popular as the eighteen-year-old Brigitte Bardot on the beach at Cannes, able to treat all men as playthings, and they couldn't get enough of me. Even the type of man you normally see sitting in a pub, happy to spend all his time with his mates taking about Arsenal could be seen outside my classroom gazing in, pitifully lost in warm feelings.

Comfort, who told fortunes, looked at my hand and said, 'You just need to concentrate on your career.' She was probably right, but which career was she talking about? Sessional teacher or diary hack? Neither felt right, and my life on newspaper diaries had opened up a new nocturnal world in which I found that the London night is as full of ghouls and grotesques as any of the prisoners' comic books.

I had to report on a party in a bijou but exclusive fashion shop in St James. It was soon as crowded as a rush-hour tube train while we waited for Kate Moss and Peaches Geldof, who might or might not show up. At the name of Kate, a vibration of excitement shot round the room as everyone hoped to get a glimpse of that famous but strange hammerhead-shark forehead, broad cheeks and tiny child-like nose, like an upside-down number 7. In the new folk religion of celebrity, she was its most sacred effigy: in puff-ball, tulips, bows, feathers, gold sandals or simple jeans, she attracted worshippers young and old, as if just to get near to her, to feel her sweet breath, might bring the elixir of youth and happiness.

She didn't turn up and while we waited I got talking to an elderly man with white bouffant hair, red face and a nose like a pen. He wore an expensive pin-striped suit and told me about his tailoring business and how he had once dressed Michael Caine and Terence Stamp. As neither Kate nor Peaches appeared, I made to leave, and he asked me to perform a sexual act on him, right then and there, amid all the traffic of people.

'Go on, please, I haven't had anyone hold my dick for so long,' he whined.

I walked down an empty Oxford Street to a bus stop, clutching my goody bag, feeling as if I had been knocked about. A week later, I saw him again at another event, stepping past, stiff as an ageing cockerel. He saw me and his eyelids flickered for a second before he bobbed away into the great bursting gut of the room.

In prison, men were not rude to me – not allowed to be, and I could throw them out if they were – but they didn't want to ignore or slight me.

'I'd go to the ends of the 'erf for you, Miss,' Julius said to me one day as he helped me to stick up some art posters. 'I mean it. I want to see you when I come out. Can we? I only come here because of you. I should be in anuvver class.'

I pretended not to listen. 'Can we meet outside sometime? 'av a coffee, Miss? Can we?'

The answer was always no. I could see that he was in some ways a lovely person, a real hoot, and I'd have loved to have coffee with him some time, but his intensity was alarming.

'They are just bloody randy,' said a friend. Whatever the reason, prison made men gracious and courteous and I wasn't unhappy about it. Almost every day I saw women of a certain age emerging into the green corridor after classes, their eyes gleaming like neglected cats that had been attentively stroked.

The men mainly wanted to keep their heads down and get on with their bird, but they could not always control their emotions. Love, for family, friends or teachers, really does laugh at locksmiths, one of the few ways to transport oneself beyond prison walls, providing some kind of hope.

There was always gossip about romances between male and female officers, female officers and inmates (some of whom did get together successfully), women teachers and students. Regardless of the risk, I soon found I was walking down the dirty green corridor and into the small dusty classrooms, hoping for a glimpse of a green Barbour or the shadow of the 'Big Dutch' on the wall. I started dressing differently: from looking like an art teacher/unreconstructed feminist/bag lady – 'scruffy' as Moose had put it so accusingly – I took to wearing a chic black dress brought from Ghost some time ago.

'You look very beautiful in black,' said Tony one afternoon at the end of a class when we were suddenly left alone for a few minutes. He spoke quietly, with dignity, and I knew he meant it.

'I am in mourning for my life,' I said. He didn't recognise the quote from Chekhov, and it sounded pretentious. It would have been better to have said nothing. But, to my surprise, he seemed to really respond.

'You must not say that. Your life is just beginning,' he said, and went out to join the rest lining up to be searched. I didn't want him to tell me about my life, which he knew nothing about – in fact, he never asked me a single question about it. Much of what we said to each other sounded fatuous, as if we were writing postcards or sending goodbye messages down a terrible phone line. But despite our basic inability to communicate on any satisfactory level, I put on make-up, including blush powder, something I only usually bother with in the evenings. One day, he stared at me close up.

'Look at you smiling so shyly,' he said, very tenderly. 'And why are you all dusty and pink?'

I knew I was going too far but couldn't stop, and of course the other men got the effect of all this too.

'Lipstick, Miss! Lipstick!' they'd shout and hoot. You wear something to slay one man and a thousand others come to the funeral. They responded very strongly to women wearing perfume, I never did so, but then I didn't really need to as it seemed that I was oozing pheromones. Bill reappeared from his barbering course suddenly and scrutinised me like a soft, round but rather dangerous cat. 'You are wearing a lot of black suddenly,' he said. 'In mourning are you?'

I never thought about Tony discussing me with anyone else. Did they while away the evenings before lock-up, discussing the conversations of the day, talking about us? I didn't know that Tony and Bill even knew each other that well, but, of course, this was not ordinary London, it was a select suburb where everyone knew everyone else, and drug dealers certainly spied out other dealers, weighing them up for size and power.

Young Mr Foch appeared in the art room at a new time, rather than going to his normal workshop. He chatted to me more than usual. Sex was in the dusty air and I was putting it there. I had told him in the past that he could have found work as a fashion or photographic model if he had made the effort. I also told him about the young Latin gigolos I used to see in Stringfellow's club in Covent Garden – how they lined up along the main bar waiting for rich, lonely ladies to buy them drinks and take them home. That was in the 1980s, when I had been rich in money and men.

'You could do that job, Mr Foch,' I said playfully.

'I could disguise myself and pull you, Miss,' he said.

'You'd be disappointed,' I said. 'I'm not rich anymore.'

'I don't want money,' he said, gazing at me and smiling confidently. 'I just like fucking.'

We were veering towards the edge of destruction but I couldn't stop. It's not every day a beautiful twenty-something says things like that, and I had begun to enjoy the danger.

'Have you ever had a younger man?' he went on. I couldn't think of any. I had certainly never bought one in Stringfellow's. While this conversation went on, Mr Smith was happily hunched over his bars of soap, and Deano was painting the face of Tutankhamen. Everyone seemed happy, and we'd got a waiting list for the class as long as Groucho's. But I was aware that it wasn't good for them to be listening to such banter.

Vere's painting of the tailor's dummy nude in the hat and some of Mr Smith's soap sculptures were selected for the Koestler Exhibition, an annual event where prisoners display their art work. The soap pieces were also put on show at the ICA Gallery in the Mall. Mr Smith's mother was invited to go along and see the work. All the teachers could go if they wished. I was interested in meeting Mrs Smith, but we were advised that Security would not allow us to have any contact with her.

BBC News decided to do a small feature on the Koestler Award, and a camera crew arrived in the art room. I put on some lipstick – entirely for Tony, but everyone thought it was because I wanted to be on telly. Then Kantila told me I couldn't take the afternoon class as the BBC didn't want any staff in there. I was required to cover another class where the teacher was away.

'But I will need to go into art to get everyone settled,' I said to her, not adding, 'and by the way, I must see him.'

Rather exasperated she said I could take two classes at once if I liked, even though they were at different ends of the corridor. I decided to do this, even if it meant running between them. Fortified by strong tea, I went first to the art class. Tony came in after the rest and ignored me. I felt a tearing anxiety start, but then he looked at me and smiled, making a small flirtatious movement of one eyebrow, and I felt righted again.

The BBC camera crew arrived, along with Kantila, who ordered me out but remained there herself.

'She wants to be famous. You should be in there, not her, you are much prettier than she is,' said Tony, overdoing the flattery rather, playing us off against each other, as he thought. He followed me out, and we walked down the corridor towards the barred gate together. Because he was beside me, the floor seems to turn soft and cloying as if I was ploughing through something like mud, my legs too weak to move easily. We seemed to be in slow motion, but, within a few minutes, we had reached the end of the corridor and an officer lounging in his chair, apparently asleep. We stood facing each other in silence, then both raised our hands to touch fingertips. Just at that moment, the officer opened his eyes and stared at us. We jumped apart and I rushed off to my other class who were waiting patiently for me.

I had nothing prepared for them, and the only film I could find was *Sweet Sixteen* by Ken Loach, which is spoken in deep Scottish dialect. The last time I saw the film, it had subtitles but these had now vanished and I couldn't get them back on. In the class were four Africans and five Jamaicans. None of the men could help, and there was no sign of any officers apart from the officer who was guarding the gate.

Africans and Jamaicans generally dislike each other, but while I struggled to get the subtitles on, they began a meaningful discussion about AIDS. The Africans said they thought it was transmitted from monkeys to men but didn't know how. The Jamaicans believed it was a virus deliberately concocted by 'them', the powers that control everything in Washington, who had deliberately injected it into the brothers to reduce their numbers. I have heard this same theory used to explain alcoholism and drug addiction in Harlem. I knew this conversation would keep them occupied for hours.

A large middle-aged African, a companionable type, said to me, 'When I am in motion, so to speak, I just cannot put a condom on. It doesn't work for me at all. Why is that, do you think?'

I did not want to talk to him about such matters, and sitting in the stuffy, darkened room, with the screen flickering and the men chatting, I realised that I was getting myself in a mess over Tony and that it could not end well. But as soon as I could I escaped back to the art room for a few moments. I found Tony spluttering and indignant about the way he had just been treated by the BBC.

'He wanted them to put him on telly,' sneered Mr Smith. 'He kept flapping a load of letters at them.'

One was headed 'My father in Venezuela' written by his sixteen-year-old daughter. Apparently a Dutch television company had made a programme about children whose parents are in prison, and his daughter was filmed visiting him in gaol in Colombia. At that time she hadn't seen him for two years.

'She was all emotional,' he said, chuckling sentimentally.

It was true, as Mr Smith said: he wanted the BBC to feature him in their programme and make him famous. He told us proudly in his big, soothing voice that he had been in prison in the Americas, North and South, Spain and Holland – and of all of them, he said petulantly, the Scrubs was the worst.

I scuttled back to my other class. They had stopped talking about AIDS but had moved on to female circumcision, which the talkative African said was necessary 'for cleanliness'. I was glad to have missed most of that one, and I sat with them trying to make constructive conversation, while inside I felt as if I was sinking. Tony was vile. It was against prison rules. And sexual attraction makes me feel so ill – rather like food poisoning.

The great clairvoyant Madame Marie of Finchley once turned up a tarot card for me showing a heart stabbed and punctured by long staves.

'You've certainly had a few ups and downs, Dearie,' she'd said. I didn't want that stupid incorrigible heart to be mine, but it was. At free flow, I rushed back to the art room as all the men were streaming out, hoping to catch a glimpse of the green Barbour. Its wearer was still sitting inside, his large shoulders hunched, a stolen paintbrush sticking out of one sleeve. Bill appeared from the cupboard, gave us a rancourous look and went out.

Tony showed me a photo of the Rembrandt House in Amsterdam. 'You were there, I know,' he said soothingly. 'I once had all the catering for a big place just across the road from there.' He made an expansive gesture. Was he once a Mr Big in catering then? I had a brief moment of hope. No, he wasn't. He meant the black woman, whom he carefully called 'the mother of my children', once worked in a café across the road from the Rembrandt House and used to let him sneak in round the back for free meals.

'Such beeootifool salads, so much sooop, wonderfool bread,' he said, like a great, guzzling grub. He was fat, prison-pallid, unclean, with unwashed hair scraped back in the style of old lags and Country & Western singers. He never cut his hair in prison as he said it brought bad luck.

'You look derelict,' I said, meaning 'for God's sake do something with yourself.'

He pretended not to know the word and started looking it up in his Dutch dictionary. 'We don't have that word in Dutch,' he said. 'It's not a proper word; at least it's not the right word.'

'Why don't you think more about your future life, what you are going to do when you get out of here?' I said.

'I don't have a life,' he said. 'Only present situations.'

'Be more responsible about your situations, then.' He had turned me, or I had allowed myself to be turned, into a mother as well as a teacher.

'You think I should try to be more selfish, think more about what I want to do?' he replied, totally disingenuous.

I should have said, 'I don't think that is possible,' but I didn't. I lost my sarcasm because I was no longer in charge. I had entered that phase where you keep quiet a lot of the time, not because there is no spark between you but because there is too much and you are in danger of bursting into flames.

Everyone had gone. Free flow was nearly finished, but he was still sitting there as if he owned the place – a man in control of his own use of time. He was risking being hauled off to the block by not going out obediently with all the rest. Perhaps he had bribed the officer on duty.

I wanted to say to him something like, 'I just want to see you alone,' but it came out as, 'I see you want to be alone,' and forced by some invisible cue I left the room. I went home feeling full of lust, but after a few hours this had turned into revulsion. As I sat at home, my image of his face changed: the small wart by his left eye looked like a cabbage; his smile was conniving and ugly (he was missing some teeth after all his years inside). He suddenly looked to me like one of those ageing vagrants that go round with a battered-looking dog on a bit of string.

When I first lived in South London, my flatmate's mother took up with a man she met while doing voluntary work at a shelter for the homeless. He had white hair in the style of Elvis, sideburns and a greying Zapata moustache. His toothless smile was a leer, and he'd swagger down the street in his Levis held up by a snake belt – the stonewashed cloth emphasising his bent old spindle-shanks. How I had despised her – but now I was turning into her.

I recalled Comfort telling me how she'd once opened the teachers' stationery cupboard in the staffroom to see a teacher and a prisoner in there 'going hard at it', copulating among the graph-paper exercise books, cheap pens and folders. The teacher was shortly afterwards dismissed.

I didn't fancy that kind of thing at all.

Some relationships formed in prison lasted – at least for a time. But with a man like this? I reflected that I would never be able to introduce him to friends, especially the ones who were now anxious older parents. They would surely consider him highly noxious to their little ones. You couldn't travel with him, at least if it meant passing through airport security. You couldn't even trust him not to steal from you.

That night, there was a perfunctory report on the *BBC News* about the Koestler Award, showing the back of Deano's head for a second but none of his work. The rest was set in the ICA Gallery, showing work by prison artists mostly from Liverpool, which somehow always remains trendy and 'cutting edge'. The report made no mention of the fact that the Learning and Skills Council had just lopped £45,000 off the budget for the award because they couldn't test or measure any of its benefits.

In the evening, I was too tired to do any painting of my own. The mournful bovine voice of Elvis singing 'Are You Lonesome Tonight' mooed from Capital Gold. I was left with my usual night-in companion, Radio 4, which can be as unreliable and dud as some of the dates I've had. Now I was working with disadvantaged people it also seemed irritatingly utopian.

That night, it offered a program on the future Olympics, presented by a relentlessly jocular disabled presenter. He told us, almost crying for joy, that Neeha Dhabi, supported by parents Rajah and Lily, may soon be set to 'end the white male domination of English swimming'.

Every one of the young people in the interviews that followed were black or Asian but, refreshingly, this concocted stew of teenagers all seemed reluctant to get involved with the plans being drawn up for them for sporting prowess. Despite the presenter's tendentious attempts to make them say otherwise, they obviously didn't want to use the Ilford running track in the evenings or plunge into the Leytonstone pool every morning at 6 a.m.

The piece was followed by a feature about Soweto Kinch, a privately educated Oxford graduate, who was about to receive £30,000 from Birmingham City Council for a music project to fund his thesis that England in the eighteenth century contained 'thousands of black musicians'.

In the interview, he offered no evidence for this assertion, and no one asked him for any. Some of his students interviewed about the project believe that Liverpool at the time was full of slaves and slave-catchers. No one contradicted them either.

I decided to tell the men about this the following day, to stimulate some discussion. I would sometimes try them out on issues around what I see as the great scam that is multiculturalism in the capital. They rarely read *The Guardian*, and very few of the British-born men followed politics at all. They'd just laugh uneasily when I told them about people like Kinch, as if it was all beyond them. Socially, they were miles removed from the new black satraps.

'You don't need to steal money: just go to your town hall and ask for it,' I once said to Deano, who looked at me curiously.

They knew that white people, even the extreme liberals, had an agenda of some kind, and, like children, they'd never heard of black quangos like 1990 Trust, which received hundreds of thousands from County Hall and purported to represent people like them. They knew nothing of the heavily funded Black Londoners' Forum or the 'Equanomics Foundation', were oblivious to £200-a-night hotel rooms funded by London taxpayers in the name of better race relations, peculatory foreign trips and false accounting. Their crimes had been much simpler, more direct, and easily found out.

On these empty evenings, without even *The Moral Maze* to cheer me up, turning over the issues of society and the hopeless lives of many offenders, I felt oppressed as if I were carrying too much alone, and I despised myself for not being more hard-headed or just harder. Prison is a place where every vulnerability gets tested.

I would have liked a companion to make my life in London less raw and to share the experience of prison. Of course, there was always computer dating. I had considered trying it; others I knew had done it with varying degrees of success, but it seemed to work better for men. Women had less luck. Take doctor's assistant Amie Huguenard, who went to the yearly Conference of Ideas in Boulder, Colorado, looking for an interesting man. Her dream came true when she met naturalist Timothy Treadwell, fell in love and lived happily with him. He took her on a romantic weekend break to the lovely Katmai National Park in

Alaska, where they were both killed and eaten by a grizzly bear, who assiduously stashed bits of them away for winter. Tim's last words to her were 'Hit it with the pan.' That's dating for you: a grisly business.

By the time I switched on the *10 O'Clock News*, the image of Tony Ten Boom had returned to my mind in all its blond beauty, swelling up to blot out all my negativity. I knew I would see him at the evening class, only eighteen long hours away.

Although it was dangerous, sometimes I had to talk about him. After I saw him chatting to a young woman teacher, the prettiest on the staff, I had to ask her about him, to check that she was not interested in him as well. She laughed so mockingly when I mentioned his name that I felt reassured. Sometimes at lunch I longed to tell Fran what was going on, that I was now 'on secret terms with con victs'. She would not have liked any infraction of the rules and, besides, she was from that generation, ten years before mine, for whom everything was political, to be put through the feminist-Marxist mincer.

After I had called him derelict, I didn't see Tony for several days, and I sensed he would take some retaliatory action. At my next evening class, I looked out for his bulky, square shoulders approaching, but he didn't come.

'Oh he's not coming,' said Mr Smith, settling himself down with his pile of soap. 'Have you been to my exhibition yet? People are going to start buying my work. I am a star.'

Men appeared, but I could hardly be bothered with them, the music or with any of it. I knew Tony would do this, and it felt bad. He had once said to me, 'I always come to your class, always make the effort to get there in the evening because I want to see you.'

He said that as if he were offering me some gift, but his words immediately opened up the possibility that he might not come. He represented constant uncertainty. I saw that the whole thing was predicated on one day his just not being there anymore. I could only think about it in the way a child might think about old age and death: a fact, but not something that could be properly thought or imagined.

'He isn't coming,' continued Mr Smith, without looking up, 'because he says he's got a bad back, but you should have seen him in here dancing about when the BBC were in, trying to get them to notice him.'

'What about Mr Portman?' I said lightly.

'No, he can't be bothered,' Mr Smith replied. 'I wouldn't come up either, only it's so boring in my cell.'

I felt angry with him, sitting there, hunched up like an old man, his long pointed nose bent low over his soap.

Strangely Tony really liked him. 'I love that guy so much,' he once said, referring, I think, to Mr Smith's utter oddness, his unswerving bleakness and pessimism. I knew they were friends of a kind, living in adjacent cells, sharing tobacco.

I rallied and worked very hard, giving everyone a lot of attention. Once I managed to get going the men were worth the effort. Secreted away, I also had a strictly forbidden item. Inside a tin with the Queen and the Duke of Edinburgh on the lid, I had some tiny fairy cakes with pink icing and a sugar rose petal on the top of each, made according to my grandmother's recipe. When we had a break, I watched as even the toughest of prisoners fell on those pink, sugary delights. As they stuffed them in, they become boyish, sentimental, relaxed. You should never underestimate the power of good English cake. Even AJ got down from his stool to take a little cake, happily skimming off a blob of icing with his tongue. We were like a good club, despite absent friends.

Making supper when I got home, I told myself that I had to start concentrating on the men again, paying more attention to their needs, but by the time I got to bed I could only think about Tony, my sensible resolution all rubbed out.

11

There was a somnambulant quality about teaching in a prison. Teachers frequently didn't show up, classes were cancelled and the prisoners didn't expect much from us, or anyone. When teachers did show up, they were often fighting entropy, in themselves and the men.

To try and move things a bit, or just to change the same dull old fare, Gerald started a history class. This was quite daring, as history was never mentioned as an academic option and we sensed that it was not really quite approved, because of ethnic sensitivities, because of the teaching profession's dislike of seeing Britain as a nation-state with an island history all its own and because its teaching outcome was not really 'measurable'.

It was gradually getting pushed off the map, like foreign languages and Classics. To give it the semblance of a proper course, Gerald ordered a new textbook from a series called 'Discovering the Past for GCSE'. Seeing a GCSE textbook for the first time was a shock. It looked like the history books I'd had at primary school: all glossy coloured pictures and very simple text and, most glaringly, no big or even medium-sized words. A chapter on the development of British law did not even include the words 'habeas corpus'. The reason for this was explained in the front of the book where it said that 'the wording of some documents has been adapted to make them accessible to all pupils.' The wording of the whole book around the documents had also been designed to the same end. This was the 'inclusiveness' they kept on about at college. Everyone would be able to read every book, and everyone would have the same small vocabulary.

Largely innocent of political correctness, or the ideology of 'inclusiveness', the men loved stories about English kings and their battles. They preferred hearing about great, charismatic individuals and dynastic struggles rather than social movements.

I was sure I could use a small amount of history to get them looking at Shakespeare's Kings, a real way of embedding literacy. None of the men, apart from one Estonian and a few Africans, had any idea of the chronology of English history and we were rather frustrated by this, so like a real old-fashioned teacher, I threw some mnemonics out to them like lifelines: 'No Plan Like Yours To Study History Wisely', with the first letter representing an English dynasty, culled from my mother's schooldays in the 1930s. When I went through that one on the board the men racked their brains to remember anything about the royal houses, but none of them had any idea about any of them, apart from the Tudors, which had recently been a popular subject for soft-porn television serials.

The Africans were fascinated by dynastic struggles, working-class movements and economic imperialism. They were also strangely interested in Scotland and all things Scottish.

A young Angolan asked me if I could find him a concise history of Britain from 'the start' to the twentieth century. This was surprisingly difficult. The library had history books about every nation in the developing world but nothing concise about the UK. I gave him my own copy of *Rhyming History of Britain, 55 BC to AD 1966* by James Muirden. Then the others wanted it, so I had to start photocopying.

The GCSE textbook had meagre amounts of information which I supplemented with downloads from the Internet and more lumps of memory from my A Levels.

We easily cut through the book's themed subjects. Crime and punishment fascinated the men, particularly the chapter on the Romans. The history of the trade unions bored most of them, and when we got to the Suffragettes, with the drawings and photos of well-born ladies in Ascot hats being hauled away by burly policemen, they fell about laughing.

One Geordie lad was highly amused at the idea of women taking over the transport system during the First World War. 'They would a had a lot more accidents then, Miss, ho, ho, ho.' I ought to have disapproved of his automatic sexism but I found him too funny to get upset about it.

I had come a long way from the firebrand feminist I once was, around about the time when I took my A Level in history, when I walked out of a class banging a desklid down because the other pupils in my Midlands comprehensive had been anti-Suffragette.

Some of the men lost interest quickly if you didn't ply them with juicy facts, but generally they loved history. One of them even wrote a poem later, referring to our history class as 'The Wormwood Scrubs Academy'.

As the classes got going, literacy kept poking through, as I hoped. One afternoon, to my absolute delight, by some miracle the Geordie lad said the name 'Tennyson'. I mentioned 'The Charge of the Light Brigade', and their ears pricked up. We couldn't find its location on the classroom wall map and I had to rack my brain about the Crimean War, why the charge was made, who gave the fatal order and how it was misinterpreted. Although I had once been interested enough to read a book on it, standing in front of the class I couldn't remember a word about it, except that someone had 'made a blunder' – but who? I distracted them for a few minutes by pointing out all the gallant garments that came from this conflict, but the Africans had never heard of balaclavas, no one could remember ever seeing a raglan sleeve and they weren't great on cardigans or even wellingtons. I knew that Lord Cardigan had led the charge on his gallant horse Ronald, but the even more gallant Captain Nolan of the 15th Hussars, the best horseman in the country, had willfully cut across him, waving his sword, and had his chest cut open by a shell splinter. All I had were these colourful, filmic moments.

By the next class I was ready with two tapes, one of Tennyson himself reading his famous poem, and a recent version read by Anton Lesser.

I asked one of the prisoners, a professional actor, once a member of the prestigious Questors Theatre in Ealing, to read it for us. There were a few actors in the Scrubs at the time, some of them quite well known and well connected. They went about looking stunned and apologetic. They had been incarcerated over a mysterious case where they were accused of kidnapping another actor. One of them explained that the man in question had been 'really annoying everybody on set', so they had locked him in a shed overnight. That kind of tomfoolery can get you into a lot of trouble these days, as they had discovered.

They were wonderful to have in class – often the only students well educated in English – and it could be unnerving to suddenly be questioned or corrected by someone with perfect vowels.

After historical work, we spent an hour on the text of the poem downloaded from the Internet, then the Geordie boy revealed that he hadn't meant Tennyson at all. He had really wanted to read 'that poem about the crow.' Did he mean Ted Hughes's 'Crow', 'The Twa Corbies' by Burns or possibly Poe's 'The Raven'?

'I like Poe,' he said, 'not this other bloke we're doin' now. I can't stand him. Can we go to the library to see if they have got it?'

Donna doesn't order much poetry, but then they all wanted to go to the library, and I was happy to go along with it because Tony would probably be there. When he saw me, he blushed a kind of dark red and opened his mouth to speak. I ignored him for as long as I could to concentrate on looking for some Poe.

'There is not usually any call for that kind of thing,' said Donna in her piercing voice, spouting crumbs.

When I went over, Tony stared up at me, and I stared down at him, as if we were trying to find some reality to the other person we had conjured in our fantasies. Sexual attraction seems to obliterate the face of the loved one, making it swim before the eyes. Peering down at him, trying to fix what I could see, was like looking at a Rembrandt close up when all you can see is an indistinct blur of gold, ochre and flesh pink.

He gave me his chair and we sat squeezed up together again, pretending to read the papers. Donna eyed us but went off to her toaster.

'I wanted to come to your class last night, but they came and raided my cell,' he gabbled in a whisper. 'I had to strip naked. They gave me a . . . ' He made some horrible hand gestures as if his body was being pulled apart.

'The search was in the afternoon. You could have come later,' I retorted.

'My back was terrible,' he started off, in a whiny voice.

'You didn't come because you wanted to hurt my feelings,' I said.

He dropped his eyes and blushed again. 'Yes,' he said, 'perhaps that is true.'

'Do I upset you?' I asked after a few moments of silence.

'Sometimes,' he said, not looking up. 'I think about your breasts all the time. You have no idea. You can't imagine what that bit of paper tissue you keep down the front of your dress has done to my mind.'

Hardip appeared and squatted next to us as there weren't enough chairs. Tony lumbered off to the inmates' loo with a copy of *Private Eye* I'd given him and didn't come back for fifteen minutes. I felt stressed and annoyed by this absence but tried not to show it as Hardip was very observant.

Tony reappeared and spread out *The Guardian*. Something was wriggling between the pages, a cockroach; the men gathered round, looking at it and me expectantly as if they thought I might scream or faint. From her cubbyhole, Donna peered out, wondering about the kerfuffle.

'Don't kill it,' someone shouted while I carried the paper and its kicking contents over to the window and, turning the paper sideways through the bars, tipped the poor thing out. I returned and whacked Tony over the head with the rolled-up paper. He took hold of it. I didn't let go and felt his expansive hand tightening its grip. We struggled, men cheered, he won the struggle but suddenly fell back against a bookcase and rolled onto the floor.

Donna emerged and waddled slowly over to where he lay like a dead Norse god.

'Can you pick him up please?' I said to her and she looked horrified, disgusted, as if the thought of touching a prisoner would be almost the same as handling a cockroach. Her reaction to the men was very different to mine as she seemed to see them as part of another, rather loathsome species, while a lot of the time I saw them as schoolboys.

When we'd settled down again an Irishman obligingly perched on the table while I drew his portrait, pretending to concentrate on him but listening to Tony.

'I want to stay in London, near you,' he said, 'but I don't know what I can do, how I can do it.'

I suggested he could become a window cleaner, as he had done that previously and in prison.

'I won't work,' he said flatly. 'They can't afford me, no one can.'

'Well, what do you want to do when you get out of here?'

'Bring about world revolution,' he said. 'Fight against George Bush, America, Britain and their war machine.'

One morning, through the narrow bars of a window, I saw his blond head and tall square figure in its green prison Barbour, walking along at the end of his gardening shift. He had a look of exquisite humiliation on his face as if he really shouldn't have been there carrying out lowly work with those people. He knew he was special and the world owed it to him to recognise it.

The next time I saw him, he whispered that he was going to be released very soon.

'I thought it was going to be today,' he said. 'I don't have to go back to Holland.' Then, rather wildly, 'I am going to come to you.' He said this almost as a joke, laughing, as if he saw himself as a threat.

Thinking about him later, I longed to touch the back of his hand, hear his voice on the phone, hang onto his ears, see him in normal clothes so that I could assess his real shape for the first time. I wondered what it would be like to sit and have tea together, perhaps at the National Gallery.

I knew we had a few evening classes left, perhaps one or two. He arrived one evening before the rest, singing, 'Should I stay or should I go? If I go there will be trouble, if I stay there will be double,' from the old Clash song. I felt a great tug of delight at the unexpectedness of it and his large, shambling masculinity.

Then they were all up, a line of turquoise prison vests and sweat pants, trooping in noisily. Mr Foch put on the radio and did a dance, there was a bit of playful kick-boxing. Mr Smith laid out his soap-carving tools that he hoped would soon turn him into a Brit Art star.

In the break, I gave out some of my special pink-iced fairy cakes. When we started drawing again Eric Clapton issued from the radio, singing, 'Darling you look wonderful tonight.' The background music suddenly became the foreground, and although they were still concentrating, the relaxed enjoyment shifted up a notch to an intense level of pleasurable longing, regret and the joy of romantic memories. As it faded there was a deep collective expiration of breath and Tony uttered a soft contented curse.

Just as we were shuddering back to normal, the foxy nose of the ginger warder appeared between the art-room doors before he came in, standing, arms folded, looking around as if he knew we'd all been up to something. He stared contemptuously at AJ on his perch then bellowed 'free flow', as if we were all deaf.

It was as if his voice woke us, and they trooped away to their cheap mattresses, Tony holding a second fairy cake inside his jacket as tenderly as if it were a pet hamster.

'I won't swap it for anything. I will have it with my tea tonight like a civilised English person,' he said, smiling down at me.

He didn't turn up to his next class.

''e's goin' Friday. Bloody relief that will be, and I will get all his burn,' said Mr Smith casually, hunching over his soap. All he could think about was tobacco, those dirty little wads of prison currency. I had a slight sick feeling which I tried to ignore.

After morning classes the next day I saw Groot sitting despondently outside the staffroom. He had suddenly been banned from going in or doing any work for the staff such as photocopying. John had seen him washing the coffee mugs and told him to get out, with the words, 'Hey you, you can't come in here anymore. Get out or I'll call the guard.'

'Thank you for putting it to me in such a nice way,' he'd said and left with his dignity intact. But he was despondent, suddenly relegated to pariah-prisoner status again, with no reason given. Security wasn't just on alert because of an audit but because someone, no one knew who, had taken out an SIR against the whole Education Department. This extreme measure always led to a detailed investigation by Security. Education, and everyone in it, was now under suspicion.

The reason might have been very small, the barred gate by the staffroom left open at the start of free flow to make it easier for staff to come and go quickly. (Security did not like any gates left open.) It might have been Groot using the photocopier or even teachers not in their classrooms on time. Something had irritated someone and now the eye of Security was truly on us.

Kantila was furious. 'I wouldn't be here now if I had a choice,' she told us angrily at an emergency staff meeting. 'Believe me, if I won the Lottery you lot wouldn't see me again, I can tell you.'

This was perhaps what the College or certainly our textbooks would have termed 'unmotivating language'. As she spoke, Jailah, sitting near her, looked around the room accusingly.

'People haven't been going to their classrooms on time,' Kantila said, 'I have spoken to several of you about it. I ask you, time and again, to be in your classrooms ten minutes before class starts, but it never happens. From now on, every teacher must be in their class and waiting ten minutes before free flow, and they must not leave the classroom for any reason until the lesson is over.'

An almost palpable wave of resentment buffeted Kantila, but she was oblivious. If Gerald had been there he might have asked if we were going to be paid for this extra ten minutes, but no one spoke. We were all thinking of ourselves confined to our classrooms, wondering how we were going to get things from the cupboards, fetch anything we'd forgotten or get more photocopies or books if more men than expected turned up. I wondered what I would do if I suddenly had to go out to the loo.

Marjorie piped up at last, with her clear ringing Yorkshire vowels. 'There is nothing in my contract about this,' she said boldly. 'I will be taking this up with the Union.'

Kantila then appointed 'course leaders' who would be in charge for one day a week, to help teachers stuck inside their classrooms. 'They will collect class numbers, and if you have any problems you will have to speak to them,' she said, as if explaining this new situation was a complete waste of her time.

'I will be in a helicopter, flying round somewhere above you all.' Then she swept out, with her daughter tagging behind.

At lunchtime, we had a 'team meeting' to discuss this new situation. Most of the teachers designated didn't want to be made 'course leaders' as it would involve extra work. Only Fatima looked pleased.

Then there was a lot of argy-bargy, with people cutting each other off and saying 'let me finish'. If we needed to be united in the face of a threat we weren't doing very well.

Rumour had it that Tony was leaving the prison on Friday. On Thursday afternoon, when everyone was busy, he gave me a Dutch diary with a small Delft tile embossed on the blue velvet cover. Inside were prints from paintings of Dutch naval battles, skaters, glass goblets shaped like windmills, a silver trowel used to lay the first stone of Amsterdam Town Hall in 1655 and an engraving showing a medieval musical evening in Leiden.

'Did you get that out of a skip?' growled Bill, who had turned up unexpectedly again.

I was happy with the gift, wherever it came from, but I couldn't talk to Tony at all. There seemed to be a wall of frustration between us.

Instead, I chatted to Mr O'Trigger, named after his appearance in our short class production of *The Rivals*. He had come in uninvited on the pretext of wanting to make a frame out of matches for a photo of Joseph Ratzinger, the new Pope. 'There might be a market for them in the Shankill Road,' I said, and he laughed, but he could probably sell anything anywhere. In the Scrubs, he sold tobacco all the time, seen openly doing deals.

Others on the staff helped him too. 'A wee girl in your office,' he whispered to me, 'you know the one in administration with the funny name, she has given me tobacco for one of me matchstick windmills.'

This snippet was offered to me like a small gift, a diary story I didn't want. I could see how he liked to slyly give one person away to another, assessing the situation, making tiny, almost imperceptible openings for new deals. But at the same time he was good company, and at least in art he was only framing people with matches.

'I would love to come round to your place and marry you, Jane,' he said. 'That I would.'

Young Mr Foch came over and said he would like to do the same. It was their idea of a huge compliment. Tony suddenly looked up, disturbed, almost alarmed, staring at me. I went to sit by him. 'I feel like committing suicide,' he said quietly.

Leaving prison is a traumatic time, almost as bad as going in, even for those who crave freedom and think they want to burst out through the roof of their cell.

As I sat there, he chanted some strange, repetitive words out loud, like someone who had been locked away for years. It is common enough to see people in London walking along muttering to themselves, lost in loneliness, but it is always an unsettling sight, and I realised that if he went to prison again his mind would probably fragment. He was on his way down to becoming one of those men with a dog on a bit of string.

'I want to go to prison in Asia next,' he said, as if sensing my thoughts. 'It's the only area of the world where I have not been gaoled.' Everyone laughed.

I forced myself to walk around and attend to everyone, listening to their banalities:

'I am painting this shark, Miss, out of my head, see.'

'I am doing this picture of SuperTed for my little boy.'

'I am copying this photo of my baby-mother, Miss. Can you draw the hands in for me?'

I was anticipating my own boredom when Tony was gone.

'You can't see prisoners for a year after they leave. Is that true?' he asked, as free flow started. I said that I didn't really know but I thought that was just a myth, it didn't really matter. Later, I wished I had been more decided and just said, 'No, it isn't true at all. We can meet outside.'

As he stood by the wall, looking at one of his own bright paintings, I slipped him a 5p I'd found in the street, something I always consider lucky. He squealed with boyish delight and called it something in Dutch.

I decided that if he came to the evening class that night, our last chance to meet, I would give him a card making it clear that I wanted him to get in touch. It was the kind of decision I never thought I'd make.

The evening class was all prepared and I'd brought in mini-doughnuts, toffees and a postcard for Tony, showing the double portrait of Isaac Massa and Beatrix van der Laen by Frans Hals, that consummate image of a happy union. My message on the back said, 'See you on the steps of the National Gallery, London or Amsterdam.'

AJ came up but no one else. Shorty and a few men from Narcotics Anonymous drifted in and sat smiling but no one else came. There had been another suicide, so the officers were short-staffed and could not bring anyone up.

I was boiling with disappointment, but I got AJ to lie on the table (bugger Security) and forced myself to draw him in a difficult foreshortened pose. As I worked, I told myself that everything was OK because we had already said goodbye the day before. He would write to me and we would meet in the National Gallery, in front of the painting of a lobster and drinking horn by Willem Kalf, or in Amsterdam in the room containing *Night Watch*.

On Friday morning I had my Level 2 English class, the best class. The men had been writing individual talks about famous people, recording them for an imaginary radio programme. Danny had been writing about Al Capone, his great hero. As we were settling down, with a lot of half-prepared scripts, Smith appeared at the door and thrust a large card marked 'personal' at me. I wanted him to take my card back to Tony.

'I can't,' he whispered. 'He'll be gone by the time I get back, he's going at ten o'clock.'

He looked terribly sympathetic – it felt a bit like being in a POW camp or that we were all in some secret game together. Smith, usually so odd and bitter hunched over his soap, was really a very good egg after all. Standing in the doorway with his secret package he looked remarkably normal, making eye contact, full of empathy. It obviously did him good to be sent on a mission.

Back in class, I took a sly glance at the card. Tony had painted it with bright inks and had written a poem, but it was all in Dutch, inexplicable.

The men in this class were too cool to shout, 'Miss, Miss,' but they were very keen for my attention, so I put the card back in its envelope and sat down to listen to Peter's recorded talk about the life of Alex Haley, the author of *Roots* and a biography of Malcolm X. He was usually witty and clever but his talk about Haley droned on. Ten o'clock was getting ever nearer, so I pretended to need some air and went to the little barred window. It was a sunny day, and it looked like a park out there with the shrubs and flowerbeds in front of the squat grey chapel. Beyond that I could see the far gate, where prisoners go out and of course later return.

I stood watching for the sight of Tony's broad back and golden hair, looking busy by holding a poem called 'It's the Way', written by a prisoner some months before, after he had read 'The Road Less Travelled'.

I was touched by his sense of failure:

And sorry I could not travel both
But a mind in struggle is different to most[. . .].

No sign of any movement by the gate. Just feral pigeons looking like little grey curling stones as they flattened themselves out in the sunshine.

'You really love those pigeons, Miss,' said Hardip, coming up beside me. Perhaps he really believed it.

At the moment Tony was supposed to be taken to the gate, Fran appeared and started talking at me. She said the College had decided not to employ any more teachers because they were appointing something called a 'curriculum manager' instead, costing the price of two teachers.

'They are cutting back on teachers even though there is still no coordinator for IT. More hopeless bungling,' she said. 'No consultation with us.' She added ominously that Fatima had applied for the job of Curriculum Manager and if she got it would probably be 'more unpredictable than ever'.

I pretended to listen to her, to get some air, to read a poem, to talk to Hardip, to be in charge of the class, but all I was doing was watching the gate. Nothing happened and eventually I had to return to the class and read the intro to a prisoner's first novel.

He was a very good writer of short pieces, but this seemed tedious, derivative of Raymond Chandler. I told him he was perhaps better at writing about his personal experiences, when he was natural and light-hearted. But he was determined that he wanted to be a crime writer.

Mr Alphons saved me from this discussion by asking if I would record Wordsworth's poem 'To Toussaint L'Ouverture' for his radio talk.

'I want a posh English voice, Miss,' he said, which was a surprise to me. Until then, I did not know that I had a posh voice, or that Wordsworth had written this poignant poem about Toussaint, the charismatic black Jacobin who rebelled against French rule in the Caribbean.

In the poem, Wordsworth thinks Toussaint is in 'some deep dungeon's earless den'. In fact he was dead by then. The poet tells the missing hero that he will always be remembered, that there are 'Powers that will work for thee,' that he will never be forgotten:

thou hast great allies;

thy friends are exultations, agonies,
and love, and Man's unconquerable mind.

Well, he was remembered, at least by the Level 2 English class in Wormwood Scrubs, and I think he would be fairly happy with that.

Mr Alphons also told me that when Napoleon was on St Helena, someone asked him about Toussaint, and the man whom Byron called 'freedom's son' replied, 'What is the death of one Negro to me?' I hadn't heard that before and felt shocked. Could it really be true? There were blank faces all round the table. I asked them if they thought Napoleon meant what he said, was he being cynical, or cruelly ironic about himself and perhaps about politics?

They didn't know enough about Bonaparte to answer, and Mr Alphons got angry as he wanted me to get on with reading more of his essay. He had no idea how interesting Napoleon's remark was and began to get enraged, about to get up and slam out. I could see by the way the men were glancing at me over their books and up from their writing that they thought it was eccentric to worry about Bonaparte's burblings. They had good, sharp brains, but I might as well have been speaking Greek. If only they had been given basic facts about European history they would be interested too, and willing to explore the relevance of those ideas to their own time.

At lunchtime, I heard that no one had been released that morning. At 2 p.m. I saw Groot sitting outside the staff-room, still looking dejected.

'Has he gone?' I asked quietly. He nodded and I slipped him a Ferrero Rocher, which all the men loved but couldn't afford on their pocket money.

As I waited for free flow to start, I wondered if Tony was already at Heathrow, or somewhere in London, in a hostel, some of the £40 still in his pocket. Perhaps he'd already smoked it away. Would he stay or would he go?

In the afternoon session I started a lesson on Orwell. We read his account of his time at school in Eastbourne, in Paris, in the London Spikes. It was all downloaded, photo-copied and ready, but the tiny barred room was so hot that none of us could concentrate, so we escaped to the library.

A bearded Sephardic Jew from Israel asked me to explain which paper he should tackle: *The Times* or *The Mail?* I offered him both, and after a few moments he told me that in his opinion they were 'exactly the same'. We smiled at each other. He looked interesting. There was also a black Dutchman from Amsterdam via Surinam. Men all round from everywhere, but without Tony the library had turned from a noisy little oasis into a dull place.

In the art room, Mr Smith was enraged about the good weather. 'I want it to snow, I want there to be floods,' he shouted. 'I don't care about those bastards out there.'

'That is a very bad attitude, man,' Deano remonstrated, putting down his brush, a rare fine one, probably found in Tony's cell. 'You will damage yourself inside if you think like that.'

True enough, but I understood Mr Smith's frustration. Perhaps because it was suddenly summer outside, I also felt like a prisoner, but Smith had something extra to be cross about, as he hadn't received any of Tony's long-awaited 'burn'.

'He didn't leave me any,' he whined. 'He's just fucked off.'

It was usual for prisoners to leave behind possessions such as tobacco for other inmates. I was shocked that Tony hadn't done it but told myself he'd probably just forgotten.

He had surely not 'fucked off'; he would be in touch soon. I planned to tick him off for not leaving anything for Mr Smith who had been his good pal.

Deano saw that I was unhappy. 'You should be glad your friend has gone out, he will be happy now,' he said, like an adult telling a child.

A man could be disruptive in class for two hours but if you then spoke to him as an individual, as a wise friend even, he would usually calm right down and respond in a normal measured way.

But my need to confide in the men could not go on. At home, I placed the card showing Frans Hal's married couple back on my bookshelf, like a postcard sent or received during a summer holiday that is now over and forgotten.

I was back to reality, almost, but I was glad to avoid my first afternoon art class without Tony, when I had to go for another session of Key Training. I still hadn't collected my keys and now, a year on, I had to retrain to get them.

The same officer as before took the class, but he was now renamed as a 'violence-reduction officer'.

'I remember you. You were the most enthusiastic person in the room,' he said when he saw me. I could remember only bewilderment and anxiety. He seemed jolly and affable, so I forgot that he was very much involved with Security.

A young woman, who was returning to work in the prison after having a baby, moaned about how long the training session was going to take, over two hours in a stuffy room. She said two hours was far too long.

'Anything that is worth saying can be said in fifteen minutes,' I said playfully. Mr Violence Reduction Man frowned.

I decided to keep quiet and he began his scary lecture on security, how to deal with the dangerous men who had done terrible things, followed by another hour on use of keys.

As I heard again the stuff about personal security and never giving out any details about yourself, I sat thinking how much I wished I had given out my details to Tony, and how much I wanted him to turn up unexpectedly at my place.

Back in my Entry Level English class I faced a row of slightly apprehensive faces, none of them with much English. I tried to get some grammar into them, but a tall gangling West Indian with a scrubby beard refused to take part. I knew he could do the work, he was just being difficult, so I ignored him, throwing aside all those lessons on differentiation and inclusion.

I tried out a 'summer' family general-knowledge quiz from a tabloid. It was quite easy, suited to all age ranges, with a bit of geography, history and natural history but as it went on I realised he couldn't answer any of the questions. I felt bad for him, but I couldn't be bothered to try to draw him in. I was feeling frazzled, bad-tempered and looking forward to getting away at the weekend, so I suggested he leave the class to do some one-to-one work with a support teacher. I could tell by his eyes that he was hurt by this, and he slid away looking rejected.

The other men seemed to know I had other things than them on my mind. I hadn't the energy to really engage with them, not present enough to force them to concentrate. They started to mock me, calling out 'free flow', to sound like an officer. It was a relief when the genuine shout came from the corridor and they all shuffled off.

About a month after Tony left the prison, I awoke one morning with a faint but certain feeling that I would never see him again. There would be no blue airmail letter sent to the prison for me. He had been in so many prisons, so many 'situations' – the Scrubs was just one more. Perhaps he had gone back to the mother of his children. Perhaps he was in another prison, or dead. Whatever, he had been just a chimera, part of the mirage that with all its special potency is prison love.

12

The college held a 'summer conference', announced as a day of 'multicultural feasting', lots of ethnic breads and adverts for Indian head massage and African dance but, sadly, no pearly kings, morris dancing, Cornish pasties or fairy cakes. The only aspect of British culture was a special health-and-safety meeting.

We were crammed into a small airless room, an obvious breach of safety regulations, with a poster on the wall showing Kitchener's face and beneath it the slogan 'H&S Needs You!' Indeed it did as Nigel our leader said he was on the H&S Committee which 'works well but rarely passes any decisions as we are never in quorum'.

He was assisted by Louise, who was in charge of 'Quality Development'. Once in charge of Art and Design, she still looked like an arts administrator in a long baggy linen skirt, corkscrew earrings and little-girl's button shoes, but somewhere along the line she had been junked by the unhealthy world of Art.

She informed us that 'working at height' had just been identified as a new H&S risk. This was nothing to do with driving cranes or cleaning the windows on skyscrapers, it's about storing things high up and climbing up to look for them. Soon, by law, everything on display in the workplace will have to be at eye level so we will all have to bend over or crouch down low if we want something.

That seemed somehow appropriate, but I wondered what she would do about Yoko Ono's famous stepladders which the original installation artist used to invite visitors to go up and look at messages and images pinned to the gallery ceiling. If H&S had existed in the 1960s in its current form, as a legion of Kitchener, would John and Yoko have met?

While outside in the sunshine people were giving each other Indian head massages and dancing to African drums, Nigel gave us a detailed lecture on fire extinguishers for different types of use, such as the CO_2 one to stop an electrical fire. These unwieldy things, once the popular plaything of students, are more dangerous now than previously because they used to be painted in different colours to make their functions clear but now, to save money, they only have a little strip of colour stuck on the side. Something else to worry about in the early hours.

I gained quite a lot of new worries at that meeting. It seemed that our 'fire marshals' were no longer connected up to anything that happened on what Nigel called 'the campus'. In fact, they could now refuse to 'deliver' their service if they felt that there was no one on site properly trained to deal with an emergency or even if the location of the fire was 'unsuitable'.

'More people are injured during evacuations from buildings than in fires,' whispered a man next to me in a seditious tone.

There are no longer any full-scale fire drills or checking of registers because there is no longer enough trained staff to do it. In the market economy, the world of bids and private tenders, it's cheaper to let folk fry.

'Just make sure you grab yer fags before yer ge' aht,' wheezed an old girl, and we all wondered how she'd got in.

In the afternoon, we were taken through the intricacies of RSI, HSE, PEEP, CoSHH and PAT. Don't ask me what they are, because like one of my white-van lads I wasn't really listening. But I did register that Nigel might help me with my plans for a new women's loo. He told me that the college could tell the prison what to do if it chose to, and he agreed to come in and inspect the site. But I had to get Kantila to invite him in and give him security clearance.

Back at the Scrubs, as one of Kitchener's new foot soldiers, I made an appointment to see Kantila, but standing in her tiny office I felt uneasy.

'I know the prison won't pay a penny for any new facilities here. It would have to come out of my budget from the College,' she said with her implacable gleaming smile. 'I won't do it. Why don't you go round other prisons and see what they've got? Wandsworth Prison Education Department is an old shed with a tin roof. Our department is good compared to most of the rest. They are far worse.'

I wondered what could be 'worse' than only one loo – apart from no loo at all.

'In Holloway, someone like you wouldn't even be able to use the lavatory,' she said, still smiling. Apparently, their loo is locked and needs an authorised key to enter, which is only given to the privileged few, not to 'someone like me'.

It seemed she wouldn't be inviting Nigel in.

'If you can get another loo put in here I will personally give you £100,' Kantila said as I left her office. She seemed irritated that I had even suggested it. As if that somehow put her in a bad light.

Back in the staffroom I felt despondent until Gerald appeared, his jaw jutting. 'I've spoken to Kantila,' he said. 'Nigel from the college will be coming in. This is a union issue now.'

He had rescued me, or so we hoped. I felt like giving him 'big hugs'.

I decided to take the final part of the teaching certificate. The thought of writing about largely pointless educational theory was not appealing, but realistically with that bit of paper I could get a job anywhere, as long as I was not considered too old. I also decided to pick up my prison keys at last. Life would be much easier with them jangling at my belt, and I would look like someone who really fitted the job. I wanted to belong in the Scrubs. It was a hole, but it was my hole.

Sometimes I allowed myself to think about Tony. Walking to work in the early morning through the leaden dust of East Acton, he would spring to mind. In the smelly loo I looked at the horoscopes in the *Metro* free paper of 15 August 2007.

Tony's Aries said, 'Remember your friends and family? They're still there waiting.' Mine said, 'It's a loved-up day, wonderful for dealing with horrible work moments because you know you've got someone who adores you.' It seemed almost marvellously wrong.

Halfway through my art class, Rod's Mr Punch profile appeared beside me. 'I need to see you later,' he muttered nervously. That made me most uncomfortable, going right back to 'See Me' notes on school maths books. His visit was also hardly necessary as I always saw him in the office at lunchtimes. It was a symptom of what Marjorie called 'psychological terror', used by Management to keep the teachers in their very lowly place.

Rod's message was that Security had decided not to give me any keys, no reason given. Had a blue airmail letter arrived from Tony after all, perhaps saying something compromising? I so wanted that to be the reason.

Tentatively, I asked Fran about letters from former inmates. She said that sort of thing would be an 'entirely different disciplinary procedure.' 'If they haven't sent for you, don't worry,' she said. 'You didn't upset them at Key Training did you?'

I wished that I hadn't said anything about keeping lectures down to fifteen minutes. That was not the sort of cheek they liked.

Fran was worried about other things. Danny had just been moved, no reason given, to a top-security prison, where he was surrounded by men who had committed bad murders. 'One of them had a body under his bed in his cell,' his brother expostulated. 'He is stuck with a load of nutters and it's doing his head in.'

She was worried about the brothers, who both being inside could not hope to see each other again for years, but we hoped Danny would fight back using his brain, writing letters and contacting the right people until, eventually, he would end up in the appropriate prison again, probably back in the Scrubs.

The day after I was turned down for keys I had another horrible work moment. I was taking the register in an English entry class when Fatima burst in to check my class list in her new role as 'teacher in charge'. She shouted something. I couldn't understand what she said, it sounded like another new acronym.

She was looking for an African student, but he wasn't in my group. As I spoke, she leaned down and screamed the name into my face several times then seemed to rear backwards, eyeballs rolling, long white teeth flashing, the image of a spooked horse. Then she walked out. The prisoner trailing behind her gave me a contemptuous sneer, picking up his mood from her.

In the short silence that followed, I felt breathless. The men stared at me and fidgeted.

'We get treated like that by the guards,' said Piet. 'It's like that on the wings.'

'She must have an unhappy home life,' someone else said, attempting to support me.

I went on with the class, but a feeling of distress kept breaking inside me, making me draw in my breath. After the class I told Fran what happened, but she was nonchalant. 'She's like that with me,' she said. 'Just ignore it.'

I mentioned it to Gerald, but his books were almost full of teacher misery and discontent. But the men in the class reported the incident to their regular teacher, and he reported it to Gerald. Then it seemed to be taken more seriously.

Fran took Fatima aside and asked her what had happened. She denied everything I said, but she said I was 'looking at her disrespectfully'. Gerald admitted that he already had three reports of bullying against Fatima, all from white or mixed-race women teachers. Nothing had gone on the official record because he and Fran had decided that it was 'bad for the department'.

Many teachers suspected that Fatima was safe whatever she did. The idea that someone might 'play the race card' or was 'close to the boss' was enough to silence most people. 'The sisterhood', as Comfort called it. I wondered if she had been one of the people on Gerald's list who had complained, but, in her usual guarded way, she didn't say, and I didn't like to ask.

Gerald said I could take out a formal 'grievance' against Fatima, which would lead to a 'proper process' and perhaps 'disciplinary action'. I didn't want to do that any more than the others did, as it was far too elaborate and scary. 'I just want someone to tell her not to do it again,' I said, but nothing as simple and straightforward as that would ever happen.

'Be like the snake but without the poison,' said Maggie Woo, the Chinese teacher, but I was dismally aware that I was more like a paralysed mouse. If someone picks on me irrationally I get upset and, rather like being in love, look for them everywhere with dread and anticipation.

One afternoon, Mr Smith carved me a little soap vitrine. In tall, slender letters inside its frame, it said gnomically 'What Will She Do?' He sold several soaps to the ICA for £120 each. He wasn't sure where the money was, but it loomed large in his mind, forming itself into fat wads of tobacco for the remainder of his sentence and into shiny new motorbikes when he went out.

His sense of self-worth was so boosted that he decided to carve a large replica of Big Ben in soap. I downloaded images of the clock tower for him so that he could get a better look at the brickwork, finials, crockets and the roof – the bits one never really thinks about. John told me not to give him any more photocopies as he was supposed to go to the library and do some research work of his own.

'I don't do that,' Smith said in his high whine when I told him. 'I don't do research. I have people like you to do it for me. That's what you are paid for, and him. I come to art for what I can get from the teachers, not for what I can do for them.'

The men were most amused listening to this tirade and I was sure he would soon settle down again as carving soap was his life's great interest.

The next day, Friday, 24 August, at 8.30 a.m., as I entered the outer chamber, I saw Rod going in. He turned towards me. I thought we were about to say 'good morning', but he said, 'They won't let you in. Go home.'

He sounded breathless, agitated, looking pale behind his stubble. I thought he might be joking, but he wasn't a great one for quips, and standing in the dingy entrance I felt apprehensive. He said he'd come back and tell me when he had found out what was going on. I waited, leaning on the rail outside, next to the queue of haggard-looking women and their babies.

Eventually he returned, panting a little. 'No idea, can't find out,' he said, 'you'd better go.'

It was 2.20 p.m. before the College called. Myleen in HR sounded embarrassed to tell me that someone had taken out an SIR on me and that I was accused of 'trafficking'. The word was very scary. It always reminded me of the film *Midnight Express*. Was it fairy cakes, cinder toffee, old paintbrushes of my own which I sometimes gave out, the paintings from photos I'd done of their children?

The last teacher at the Scrubs found guilty of trafficking had been sent to prison for four years. She was still in Holloway, that giant crèche in North London, among the sad she-lags. But she had been caught with heroin inside a mobile phone rather than a tin of iced cakes.

HR said I would be getting a letter giving me all the details of the charges against me. An eleven-page document arrived surprisingly promptly the next day but gave no details about any charges. It said I had to go to the college for a 'disciplinary meeting' the following week.

'Just deny everything and say as little as possible,' advised Fran. 'Don't try to explain anything.'

Colleagues began to ring up, full of rumours. 'They are

paying people to spy on each other. A prisoner has been questioned. He says he has been giving out his artworks in exchange for tobacco. He has fingered you.' As I had always been a non-smoker and hated the men smoking, that one was unlikely.

Over a pizza in Notting Hill, Fran and I broached the almost unbearable subject of who had reported me. She said it was probably Fatima. I didn't want to think that Fatima really hated me that much, especially over nothing more than an expression she imagined she saw on my face.

'You underestimate the little people,' said Fran, suddenly not sounding like a socialist. 'They like to do damage.'

Comfort also blamed Fatima. 'She is obsessed with how people look. She feels safe with very dark people like herself and people who act the way she does,' she said. 'She is obsessed with skin colour. For her it has become a shibboleth, and thinking like that, being absorbed by this world of colour, it's so empty and meaningless but it can take over your mind and destroy you as a person.'

Left at home to while away the hours, I felt uneasy. Suspension doesn't feel as if you are being stretched from the ceiling by your arms, it is more like being laid down and pressed by heavy weights. It does not feel like a holiday. But fate often slaps you across the face and shakes your hand at the same time, as I suddenly had plenty of time to paint, write and read.

The papers were of Kate Moss's new hairstyle and her on-off relationship with singer Pete Doherty, overshadowing the rather duller news that prison officers had launched a lightning strike over their meagre 1.9 per cent pay rise.

The day after I was refused entry, 30,000 of them lumbered out of the nation's prisons, closing down all penal education departments in England and Wales. The new

'Ministry for Justice', which sounded as if it was culled from a novel by George Orwell, crossly declared the strike illegal, mentioning 'contingency plans' against the strikers. There were rumours that the Army would be called in, but it seemed they were too bogged down in Basra. During the strike, the governors and Security took over the Scrubs, and an elaborate system of bribery immediately went into effect. An officer told me later that they gave out sweets and tobacco to all the men and were even seen lighting their burn to keep them all quiet and happy.

'They got everything they wanted for a day,' he told me, laughing rather bitterly. 'But there will be no record of it.'

A day later, the Government announced that public-sector pay was going to be strictly controlled. I felt indignant, as part of this tribe of low-paid workers. If I had still been a well-paid feature writing tabloid journalist, I would probably have hardly noticed the strike or this announcement. In all the years I sat in Groucho's I probably socially never met a low-paid person apart from waiters.

As no one knew anything about my case, we all had to wait to see what Security decided about me. They were 'investigating' whatever had been written about me in the SIR.

I looked at my tarot cards – they are less trouble than the union and cheaper than a lawyer. I turned up the VIII: La Justice. This meant that nothing had been decided, everything was in the balance. Professor Dawkins might think that looking at cards is a very silly thing to do, but it made me feel better.

A few days after our pizza Fran phoned. 'I was so depressed about it all that I couldn't go in today,' she said. Kantila and her deputy were off, Fran and two other course directors were away, at least two teachers were off sick, and two others – apart from Simon and me – were also suspended. 'They might have to close Education,' Fran said, with some satisfaction. She said that prisoners had been coming out of their classes without permission to ask her what had happened to me. They were of course not told anything.

Apparently, most of the other teachers were not speaking to Fatima, who was referred to as 'Bitch Features' by one of them, but she was seen having big hugs with Mr Nusrat. There was a mood of fear in the staffroom, which made it hard for anyone to concentrate on teaching.

'We are supposed to be reinforcing the best in the men, and this isn't helping,' said Fran. 'People are convinced that Kantila is using Fatima as a spy – not true of course, at least I don't believe it.' The other view was that she was not interested enough in her job to employ spies.

Then she gave me a lecture: 'If you survive this, you will have to change your ways. You must not speak about anything in a light-hearted or flippant way, not say anything in the hearing of anyone in authority and not trust anyone. And that probably goes for teaching anywhere, not just in prison.'

Wit and satire, wave it goodbye. It belonged in my other life. Another week went by with bits of news, or rather gossip, filtering through to me. I heard that Vere was back inside and had given up art but taken up playwrighting, which was fairly good news. But there was also bad. It seemed that Mr Smith, the good egg, had fingered me. Of course he was upset because I refused to give him the photocopies of Big Ben. Back in his cell, brooding on this, he must have decided to accuse me of trafficking, dragging up every cake and choc I had passed him over the months. It was just as they said: you could never trust a prisoner. But he and I had a shared experience, and I did not want him to suffer.

'Nothing to do with you,' said Fran.

'Think about your own situation,' said Gerald grimly.

Fatima was seen in the corridor one day, long arms waving, shouting to Mr Nusrat, 'No one crosses me and gets away with it.'

In my new spare time, I decided to try to track down my certificates for passing Parts I and II of the City & Guilds Certificate in Further Education. Although it is a smallish college, it took me a long time to find any department that knew anything about our exam certificates. When I finally found the right extension, a foreign voice told me she couldn't find any record of the course or any certificates. In my stressed state, this almost reduced me to tears. Comfort had received her certificates for the same course she was doing in the evenings, so I knew that the course had taken place – I hadn't imagined it. In another phone call, I was told that the certificates had 'all been sent out already.' Then in another I heard that they would be 'getting them in soon'. This is England, where nothing works, and everyone from whom you need basic information is either in Delhi, Rangoon or just arrived here from the Antipodes.

Charley in IT, whose dad was high up in administration at the college, had worked in an office there for one summer. He said that most of the staff were on short contracts and did as little as possible. Filing certificates was a job no one wanted as it was so boring, so it just wasn't done. And if it was done, no one wanted to carry them into the 'right room'.

Several of us decided to phone the college, demanding our certificates and, under this barrage, they agreed to carry them to the right room and give them out. So, one lazy afternoon, carrying passport, driving license and two recent bills to prove I was myself, I wandered through bosky Brompton

Cemetery, which seemed to be having its own lunchtime free flow of men jogging and cycling in tight shorts.

Inside the administration block, which was on a different site to my usual college, I found there were no signs anywhere for the Exam Office, but the walls were lined with large notices with big blue arrows directing me to the 'prayer room'. I was reminded uneasily of some words from Pervez Hoodbhoy, Professor of Nuclear Physics at Islamabad University, who'd recently complained on the BBC that his campus now has four mosques but no bookshop.

The Exams Office turned out to be a small hut outside in the car park. A surly mixed-race girl with the same tiny head, skinny jeans and skimpy top as the girls in the prison office, frowned at me, demanded the ID, then disappeared into a locked room, reappeared, locked the room, presumably against boundless lurking cheats, put my certificate on top of a tall filing cabinet and asked me to sign it.

It was obvious to both of us that I couldn't reach up there to write, and I had to ask her to put it onto a desk in front of me. She sighed with annoyance, and there I was, the first stage to becoming a teacher completed.

Walking back through the park, a squirrel with rheumatism in its hind legs and a practised eye carefully took some chocolate from my fingers, and I realised that at my advancing age I had no work to go to and no idea if I would ever be involved in teaching again. My new career had lasted less than a year.

'If you haven't done anything, you can't be found guilty,' Comfort told me flatly, her weight and silent obstinacy supporting me.

A long week later, I went back to the college for my 'disciplinary meeting'. I was relieved to see Gerald arriving, his feet slapping loudly on the tiled floor, shaved head gleaming, obviously spoiling for a fight.

He told me what little he knew, some of it still rumour. Mr Smith had been so annoyed about the Big Ben dispute that he had decided to abandon his key-skills qualification. Fatima, as coordinator of that subject, went to the art room to see him. He mumbled some rude things about the art teachers, adding that I had given him photocopies and Simon had given him tobacco. She then phoned Kantila, who was on holiday, and told her that she had discovered something 'terribly serious going on in the art room'.

Kantila told her to take the matter to Rod the deputy, but Fatima told her he had already gone home. In fact, he was sitting in his office nearby. Believing that there was no one else there, Kantila told her to go ahead, and she promptly filled out a dreaded SIR report.

The accused Simon had been found guilty of trafficking tobacco and sacked. I was shocked. He had been there for years but given no warning or second chance.

But what had I done? Mr Smith had only mentioned photocopies, which were not banned, as yet. No one knew the charges against me, but Gerald was sure that HR would tell us.

I felt nervous as we entered the 'Child Care' room where we were meeting. The walls were covered in bright paper sunflowers, and we had to sit at a very low table on small chairs. I was facing Myleen, who looked embarrassed, and beside her the formidable Glenda Gittings, a stout blonde woman wearing lavish make-up. There was silence as we all stared at each other, and I realised they were waiting for us to start.

'Can you please say what it is she is supposed to have done?' Gerald began firmly. They looked blank, and it became clear they didn't know.

Glenda said that she believed that Kantila might know something, but she wasn't allowed to say, so they hoped I was going to tell them what was going on.

'Did you ever take anything in? Any sweets or anything?' said Glenda hopefully. I started to tell her that I had: cakes, biscuits, sweets sometimes, books, photocopies. She started to write this down, but Gerald cut me off quickly.

The formal meeting was then over and turned into mutual commiseration about the way things are being run at the Scrubs and prison education in general.

'We get a huge turnover in staff because of the stress of the place,' said Glenda.

'There is always such a feeling of being second class,' said Gerald bitterly.

'It doesn't help that you can be booted out by Security if someone takes a dislike to you,' I said, and they all looked at me with interest as if they knew I was talking about someone specific. I didn't mention Fatima, because, unless I made a formal complaint against her, she could not officially be mentioned.

'In the last analysis, things are better in prison education than they were five years ago,' says Glenda. 'But, at the end of the day, Security can do what they like. They don't need to give a reason and we can do nothing whatever about it.' To help me along, they offered me counselling through the 'college support network'.

The only charge against me was that I had given out images of Big Ben from the Internet – except that I hadn't given them out; they were still stuffed in my pigeonhole. Any new rule about internet material had been brought in retrospectively, so I was not guilty of a non-crime.

A week after this, Security got in touch to say they wanted to issue me with a 'warning'. The College said that this was not possible because the prison didn't employ me – they did. Gerald was now beside himself with indignation and wanted to take the matter to the Learning and Skills Council, the Home Office, Strasbourg and the Hague if necessary.

It also emerged that I had said something at Key Training which Security didn't like, but they wouldn't say what it was. They wanted to meet me, along with Kantila, but she was having a disagreement with the woman in charge of Security and also with Glenda Gittings, so nothing was arranged.

I went on languishing at home, fed regularly with stories from the prison. Another teacher, a young Scots girl, had complained to Gerald about Fatima for exactly the same behaviour, the close-up screaming into the face. She didn't want to risk going in for a formal procedure either, but she was taking notes of her own.

At one of the day-long 'inset' training days, a black woman teacher accused Fatima of racism, but only verbally to another teacher.

A prisoner had lobbed an apple from his cell window as Fatima was walking underneath, beaning her on the ear. She had launched an investigation, the culprit had been identified and sent to the punishment block.

On 18 September 2007, Gerald and I were invited to a meeting with Sylvia Starke, the Head of Security. On the second floor of the administration block a tiny skinny woman in a purple cardie was sitting behind a very large desk. She had hair like one of those drawings of whirlpools by Leonardo.

A moment later, a massive woman with short cropped grey hair strode in. This was Miss Starke, Head of Security. She seemed to fill the doorway, all in black from her military-style jersey, which gripped her capacious bosom, down to her large shiny boots.

'I am Head of Operations,' she said, as if we could have doubted it, and sat down, knees wide apart, leaning forwards, staring at me with one eye almost closed. I stared back, smiling slightly, a bit coquettish, which I felt was the safest way to go.

'You and me are going to have a chat,' she said, in a wheezy voice that suggested she was no stranger to Capstan Full Strength, 'like I am entitled to do. And *who* are you?' she said to Gerald with restrained contempt.

'From the Union,' he said. 'And *you* should know that the LSC are following this up.'

'LSC, whatsat?' she demanded, but as he tried to answer she cut him off. '*You* should know, that woman Gittings at the College has put my back right up. I can tell you, that's her mistake, and it won't do you any good. Education has no jurisdiction in this prison. You are on my patch.'

'Miss Starke advises the Governor,' said the little lady behind the desk.

'I am God,' Miss Starke boomed, at no one in particular.

'She advises the Governor, the top man in the prison,' the little lady repeated. 'He always listens to her.'

'If he's got any sense,' Miss Starke snorted, while Gerald and I smiled back fixedly.

I asked her tentatively about the issue of the images from the Internet, the only specific charge I had heard against me. She seemed to know nothing about it, and unwisely I tried to explain: 'I downloaded images you see, for the prisoner's art project, and now we hear that teachers are not allowed to do that.'

'Downloading images?' She didn't like the sound of that. The word 'images' was ill chosen.

'If prisoners say they are very interested in a particular topic,' I explained, 'I get the material from the Internet for them.'

'They will say they are interested,' she said, launching into something. 'That's how it all starts. They are manipulative and untrustworthy, and if they are asking you to get something for them and you are bringing it in, then that is trafficking!'

'They were images of Big Ben,' I protested. I was about to explain that most of the downloaded material was poetry or historical stuff, but Gerald was shushing me.

'We feel that this whole issue sprang from malice,' he said.

'I am only interested in security,' she replied, like a wise headmistress. 'There were security questions about Miss Kelly. I am not happy about her having keys.'

'I haven't got any,' I said.

'That's right,' she said, staring at me, her knees going even wider. 'And we are going to watch you for three months, then we may look at the situation again.'

'What did I say at the Key Training that was wrong?'

'I am not here to give you details.'

'But if I knew I could avoid saying it again . . . '

'If there was anything wrong you would not be here now,' she replied bitingly.

'If I knew what was wrong perhaps I could put it right?'

'We'll just forget the whole thing,' she said, waving her large hand, as if it had all been a misunderstanding between friends.

Outside, standing between the high wire fences, Gerald and I had a sense of having escaped something terrible.

'I think she was OK,' he said, 'quite chatty.'

'I was glad I put on a nice dress,' I said. 'Always a good idea in a crisis.'

It probably also helped that we were as blindly charming as we could be, but it was obvious that Miss Starke knew nothing about Fatima or what brought this situation about. It was a bad coincidence that I had somehow upset someone during Key Training and that Fatima's form had followed just after that.

It was also clear that the Education Department with its links to the College was also of no interest to Miss Starke.

'She was probably once just an ordinary officer,' said Gerald sadly. He meant someone who had risen through the ranks, like the Governor himself, part of a prison culture which, unlike the police, had never been forced to change.

In the few days before I got back to work, I heard a rumour that Part III of the much-desired Certificate in Education had been abolished.

'Part III has become Year 2,' said the certificate course co-ordinator. 'Depending on whether you are generic or specialist.'

I had no idea what I was, only that I was happy and relieved to still be a teacher at the Scrubs.

On 24 September, just as the weather turned towards winter, I returned through the Scrubs pressure chamber back into the prison. I could have stayed away on full pay claiming 'stress' for a lot longer, but I was glad to be back.

I wasn't so happy when I realised that Security had removed my staff pass and I had to wear the badge of a daily visitor, which meant I had to be escorted everywhere within the prison and watched at all times.

Comfort met me at the gate and walked me into Education that first morning and I felt very grateful. The man on the gate with the pipe waved me through, and I felt people were glad to see me, but my new pass was bright pink, and I thought of it as a kind of scarlet letter.

It was particularly upsetting to be stigmatised while Fatima went about as if nothing had happened. Fran reassured me that she had been 'ticked off' by the College, but not for causing disruption with a false accusation, not for malice, only for 'not following the proper procedure' when she filled out the SIR form against me. They could only pick her up on the fact that she had lied about her immediate boss not being there.

She wasn't around – 'off sick' people said – but I was on edge in case she appeared. I not only dreaded seeing her but also felt uncertain about John, who strangely had not contacted me once throughout the whole business, even though it had all been to do with the art room. He smiled when he saw me.

'Will you be in the art room today?' I asked him, thinking it would be nice to have him around on the first day.

'No, it's all yours,' he said and drifted off.

My class was still intact, apart from Mr Smith now confined to his cell, cruelly cut off from his soap. I got a warm reception, except from the remaining Atkins twin, who sat smiling unpleasantly as if he knew something really bad about me. Or it could have been a smile of admiration that he knew something bad about me, I wasn't sure. There was a lot of curiosity about where I'd been, but I wasn't allowed to say anything. Ivan was delighted to see me and showed me more remarkable drawings he'd made on the wing.

Midway through the session, Rod's unwelcome mug appeared at the door, saying that Kantila wanted to see me after class.

John was sitting in her office when I arrived. She told me that I would no longer be taking any art classes, due to 'restructuring', and from now on John was going back into the classroom. My 'cover' period for him was over. We all knew that I had never covered for him. Like the other teachers, I had been given my own classes. He sat there listening, his long face a blank, and I had the gloomy realisation that Kantila was angry with me rather than Fatima.

I was stunned at losing all my art classes and desperately screwed up some courage to find out what this was all about. I stopped John and asked him just what was going on. He seemed really surprised; like a snake snacking on a mouse, it seemed he had no idea that any action of his might cause pain. He seemed to think that nothing had happened.

'Just one of those things,' he said quite lightly, but then added with a kind of cold vagueness, 'no one told us you were coming in last September. We were all surprised that someone else was brought in and we all lost some of our teaching hours because of you.'

An explanation at last for his coolness and for the attitude of the two Simons, also perhaps for why I had been thrown into the class at the beginning and left to sink or float. It would have been so much easier at the beginning if he'd just come in a few times and helped me.

To leave journalism and enter the public sector is to refrain from telling your colleague that he is the brother of a reptile, but it wasn't entirely his fault. I could see that the people in charge were so fed up, so wishing to win the National Lottery and jet off to Barbados, that they had not bothered to tell John or the Simons about my arrival, which had led to seething resentments.

'Take no notice, teachers in here are always being treated like this,' I heard, and 'just take the money, that's what we all do.'

Management was not entirely to blame either, as it had to try to manage a department without any real power. Security controlled everything, and below them the officers.

The prison exists for them, just as the woman officer had told me as she emerged from the loo on my first day.

Mr Portman visited me the following day in one of my English classes.

'I'm depressed about all this,' he said.

I shared his feeling, as I had become very attached to the art room and everyone in it.

Ivan arrived, waving a lot of large drawings at me. There was nowhere that I could look at them, and I had to shoo him back to the art room before he got into trouble. Ivan told me that the evening class was finished: John had told him bluntly that it was now scrapped. Soon, all the other evening classes were to go the same way, making life easier for the officers.

I took the next day off because I realised that I felt as murderous towards John as any inmate in the place had ever been towards anyone.

'The amount of time that is spent here screwing each other is pitiful,' said Comfort in her phlegmatic way.

Fran was more enraged. 'All this in-fighting is time that could be spent on the prisoners,' she said, 'in the end they are the ones who always get screwed as our mental focus is always being diverted from them in order to represent ourselves in these little political squabbles. The needy and the vulnerable are being screwed by the self-serving people in this system.'

But she and Gerald were encouraging and said that the mood of heightened security would all pass. Things would settle down again. I had the final part of my teaching certificate to think about. I had to try to get to grips with it in its brand-new form with attendant new acronyms. I had also asked Yvette Khoury, a Shakespearian scholar from Oxford, to come in and deliver a workshop, and she had agreed. That was something to look forward to.

I still had my other parties at night to keep me busy. They now seemed a relief from the stresses of life as a prison teacher.

I had once been very fed up with my life as a journalist but now I welcomed the chance to work on something alone – doing it all myself without any outside interference or petty politicking from others. As a journalist, I was a one-woman show, largely invisible, watching others perform, away from any attention myself.

I was invited to a Venetian Ball at Strawberry Hill House, the Gothic mansion near Richmond. It was a *mascheranda,* of the sort they hold in Venice, where the great game of transgression and seduction is elegantly worked out in masks, beautiful costumes and historical dances. The guest list was crammed with A-listers, but I quickly realised that the great catch was that we were all masked. If it had been done deliberately to upset the press, it worked. At last the glitterati had found a way to escape from the likes of us, by simply sticking on or lifting up on a stick a bit of cardboard and tinsel.

To the music of Vivaldi, Jerry Hall and other celebs swept into the cold marble hallway, clad in Vivienne Westwood gowns. I caught glimpses of famous chins, brows and flashing teeth – the rest lay hidden behind an array of feline, feathers and pearls. The men arrived in tooled and elaborate black and gold half masks, ugly pockmarks and scars covered by silk, bald pates by horse-hair curls.

I knew it was going to be hopeless, at least until they all got drunk and discarded the disguise, so I decided to forget why I was there for once and just stay in the ballroom, which was lit by flaming torches, quaff the chilled champagne and watch the dancers, who were doing quite well in their lavish lace skirts and tight silk britches.

I was back in the drowning city, this time in the eighteenth century, where all that mattered were looks and class. It wasn't long before some of the men, like good sports, abandoned their masks. A portly old Etonian diarist pottered up to me. I liked him as he had the sort of burnished calm that only Old Money can buy. We were joined by an illustrious glossy magazine editor, also an Etonian, wearing a lopsided lawyer's wig.

They bowed low, making a few murmuring sounds, which I knew to be the opening tones of their own private language. This consists mainly of small grunts, chirrups, smiles and nods. It is charming to watch, the residue of a whole culture of manners, deference and obligation and a rarefied form of the barter and exchange system I saw every day in the Scrubs – except this wasn't about burn or drugs but contacts and advancement.

The Editor had just opened a new edition of his magazine in Bombay, the coming place. The Diarist had two daughters already doing work experience on *Tatler* and mentioned very vaguely, by means of chirrups and smiles, that his other daughter was starting her gap year and thinking of travelling in India. With no more than a murmur and a small inflection of the head, the deal was done. 'She'll want the beach for a while,' said the Editor reassuringly, 'but when she's done that and seen all sights, tell her to come into the office. Of course she can work for us.' It was simple and unobtrusive as a hand curled behind an officer's back to receive the goods.

I drifted back into the marble entrance, where the front doors were kept open for a mass of photographers still gathered there. Someone special was due, and I woke up as if water had been splashed on my face. Whoever they were, I had to try to spot them and get them to speak, with or without a wretched mask.

In the middle of the hallway were small CCTV screens, back to back on top of an ancient stone font. Looking into these we could see the gardens where the bushes and lawns looked yellow, vaporous, and I could make out the long shapes of dogs, if they were dogs, a whole lean, shaggy grey pack of them, loping lightly about as if they'd been cooped up somewhere all day and were now enjoying the dank night air. Only a few other people seemed to notice and stood around watching, fascinated as I was.

But who were they protecting, who was hiding somewhere deep in the house? It's always possible to ask a photographer, but I cringe from doing that, as they have their world and we have ours, and it is somehow distasteful to ask them for anything. But looking ahead all the time, his face hardly moving, one of them quietly dropped the names 'Kate and Pete'.

It was not a welcoming house, and I felt uneasy as I made my way through darkened hallways, all leading to locked rooms and occasional lavatories. Other passages led to small, lozenge-shaped chambers where disheveled young people lay sprawled about drunk and stoned among scattered musical instruments. They had obviously been there for some time, as if they were left over from an earlier party. It was all so unexplained that it felt like a dream.

Further in, hallways narrowed and were blocked by stocky security men in dark glasses and black uniforms. That meant I was getting nearer. I got through this phalanx of beef in tight collars by being very girly, smiling weakly, or perhaps as a woman of my age, by being totally invisible. However it was, they melted back and let me through.

I pressed on down stone passages, where the old kitchens must have been. There was hardly any light, and the ceilings were very low. I turned a porcelain door handle and, from behind it, I could hear what sounded like a big dog whining and scratching. The men in dark glasses reappeared and tried to push me back again, but they were too late because I had found them: Kate and Pete. She was sitting on the edge of a broken-down sofa, looking bored but alert, as if anxiously waiting for something to happen. He was lolling against a wall in the hallway, leaning on the mottled yellow wallpaper.

When she saw me, her long cotton gown seemed to flutter slightly, but he went on lolling and smoking absently. He was surprisingly tall, all in black, and when his round, glassy eyes eventually focused on me, he smiled and looked friendly, almost as if he had been expecting me. Kate came over immediately, regarding me with interest. It was as if they hadn't seen other human beings for years, had been cut off somehow and were both separately lonely. Perhaps they'd been quarrelling, cooped up there for hours together. I wondered why were they in that house at all, looking so unhappy. If they were not enjoying the evening, why not just go home? Perhaps the pack of photographers clustered around the front door had scared them into this lair.

Kate's triangular kitten face wrinkled up as she smiled, and she showed me her engagement ring. This was a scoop. She said it had been made especially for them – not very expensive, only £300. We all stood quietly focused on the small stone in its square setting, like something any teenage girl might have, while Pete seemed to swell with happy pride.

'We will be getting married soon, I am not sure exactly when,' she said in a sweet voice.

'It'll be when I can get myself together and really look after her,' said Pete. He sounded genuine and full of happy fondness for her. I told him I'd done some portraits of him, based on something I'd seen by Modigliani which looked very like him, and I wondered if I could paint him from life? He seemed interested and amused and gave me his phone number.

Then Kate suddenly snapped out of her dreamy state. 'Are you a journalist?' she said, looking quite horrified. I admitted it. She gave me a look of withering disappointment, arched her narrow back and stalked over to the old sofa. Pete remained there, leaning, as if he hadn't noticed anything or didn't care. I could have stayed longer chatting to him, but there was not a moment to lose: I had to get this story through quickly in case someone else beat me to it. They had both fallen silent anyway, staring into space – she unhappily with a scowl, he looking detached and tired.

I raced back through the narrow passages, over sprawled-out legs and discarded beer bottles, past endless empty rooms, out onto the freezing terrace where lanterns illuminated the shape of drunken people sitting and lying on the damp ground. A former newspaper editor, half lying on the path, raised his glass and laughed as I rushed by.

I sent the interview through to the night desk and crawled under my duvet, knowing I'd got the story I needed at last. I had been the agent of my own rescue, lashing together my own raft.

The next morning, the story of the engagement was splashed across two pages of a national tabloid, with a staff news reporter's name on it. I sent him an email saying, quite seriously, that I would kill him if we ever met, but at least I had got the story and had put it through. A hard-wired pattern of behaviour was successfully completed, a reflex and a compulsion had been satisfied. I was still a journalist after all whether I wanted to be or not.

Perhaps it was this, the pink badge or losing my art classes, but in early October I started writing about prison. Once I had begun, I couldn't stop.

'Are you an undercover reporter, Miss?' one inmate asked shyly. Some thought it was fun; others were scared of me. Undercover I was not. I started writing and no longer bothering to conceal it – even trotting around with an orange notebook.

One bright morning I walked through the inside gate, making notes as I went. Kantila's husband and the small man with the pipe stared at me in disbelief, as if I was walking through carrying an automatic machine gun. If they ask, I thought, I will just say I am working for Health and Safety, examining the razor wire for its level of risk, or counting up cockroaches.

'I am so sorry you are leaving, Miss,' said a young prisoner with beaded hair that afternoon. 'You seem like a really nice person, so I just wanted to tell you that.'

He was so sweet, but what was he on about?

'There is a rumour here that you are leaving today,' he said, beginning to look worried.

'Rubbish,' I said. 'No one has said anything to me about it.'

Half an hour later, after the class finished, I was taken over to Security. Miss Starke was seated behind a big desk. 'You are a journalist,' she said in a calm, soft voice. 'The Governor won't stand for that sort of thing here.'

Apparently, someone in the Governor's office had googled me and had seen me listed there as a journalist. Well, it had taken them a year to catch up with me.

'Number One Governor no longer wants you to have access to this prison,' she said, peering down at a pariah to be shooed off the premises as fast as possible, Shakespeare workshop and all.

I was considered so dangerous that I couldn't even return to the staffroom to collect my things or say goodbye. Moments later, I stood between the wire fences in front of the stone exit porch. The sluice gate opened, and I was expelled back out into the vast open waters of London.

Like countless others who have gone that way, I hesitated for a moment, wondering, can I go on swimming or will I simply drown?